Literary Criticism and Cultural Theory

Edited by
William E. Cain
Professor of English
Wellesley College

A Routledge Series

Literary Criticism and Cultural Theory

William E. Cain, *General Editor*

Narrative Mutations
Discourses of Heredity and Caribbean Literature
Rudyard J. Alcocer

Between Profits and Primitivism
Shaping White Middle-Class Masculinity in the United States 1880–1917
Athena Devlin

Poetry and Repetition
Walt Whitman, Wallace Stevens, John Ashbery
Krystyna Mazur

The Fiction of Nationality in an Era of Transnationalism
Nyla Ali Khan

Gendered Pathologies
The Female Body and Biomedical Discourse in the Nineteenth-Century English Novel
Sondra M. Archimedes

"Twentieth-Century Americanism"
Identity and Ideology in Depression-Era Leftist Fiction
Andrew C. Yerkes

Wilderness City
The Post World War II American Urban Novel from Algren to Wideman
Ted L. Clontz

The Imperial Quest and Modern Memory from Conrad to Greene
J. M. Rawa

The Ethics of Exile
Colonialism in the Fictions of Charles Brockden Brown and J. M. Coetzee
Timothy Francis Strode

The Romantic Sublime and Middle-Class Subjectivity in the Victorian Novel
Stephen Hancock

Vital Contact
Downclassing Journeys in American Literature from Herman Melville to Richard Wright
Patrick Chura

Cosmopolitan Fictions
Ethics, Politics, and Global Change in the Works of Kazuo Ishiguro, Michael Ondaatje, Jamaica Kincaid, and J. M. Coetzee
Katherine Stanton

Outsider Citizens
The Remaking of Postwar Identity in Wright, Beauvoir, and Baldwin
Sarah Relyea

An Ethics of Becoming
Configurations of Feminine Subjectivity in Jane Austen, Charlotte Brontë, and George Eliot
Sonjeong Cho

Narrative Desire and Historical Reparations
A.S. Byatt, Ian McEwan, Salman Rushdie
Tim S. Gauthier

Nihilism and the Sublime Postmodern
The (Hi)Story of a Difficult Relationship from Romanticism to Postmodernism
Will Slocombe

Depression Glass
Documentary Photography and the Medium of the Camera Eye in Charles Reznikoff, George Oppen, and William Carlos Williams
Monique Claire Vescia

Depression Glass

Documentary Photography and the Medium of the Camera Eye in Charles Reznikoff, George Oppen, and William Carlos Williams

Monique Claire Vescia

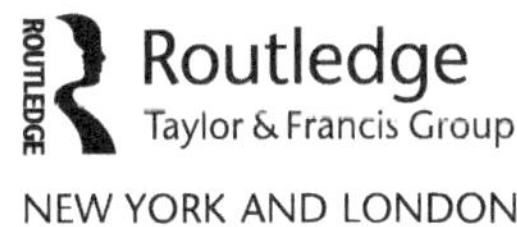

NEW YORK AND LONDON

Published in 2006 by
Routledge
Taylor & Francis Group
711 Third Avenue
New York, NY 10017

Published in Great Britain by
Routledge
Taylor & Francis Group
2 Park Square
Milton Park, Abingdon
Oxfordshire OX14 4RN

First issued in paperback 2015

Routledge is an imprint of the Taylor and Francis Group, an informa business

ISBN 13: 978-1-138-81253-6 (pbk)
ISBN 13: 978-0-415-97547-6 (hbk)
Library of Congress Card Number 2005024639

Library of Congress Cataloging-in-Publication Data

Vescia, Monique.
Depression glass : documentary photography and the medium of the camera eye in Charles Reznikoff, George Oppen, and William Carlos Williams / by Monique Vescia.
p. cm. -- (Literary criticism and cultural theory)
Includes bibliographical references and index.
ISBN 0-415-97547-6 (alk. paper)
1. American poetry--20th century--History and criticism. 2. Literature and photography--United States--History--20th century. 3. Williams, William Carlos, 1883-1963--Knowledge--Photography. 4. Reznikoff, Charles, 1894-1976--Knowledge--Photography. 5. Oppen, George--Knowledge--Photography. 6. Visual perception in literature. 7. Photography in literature. 8. Depressions in literature. 9. Objectivism (Philosophy) I. Title. II. Series.

PS310.P48V47 2005
811'.520912--dc22 2005024639

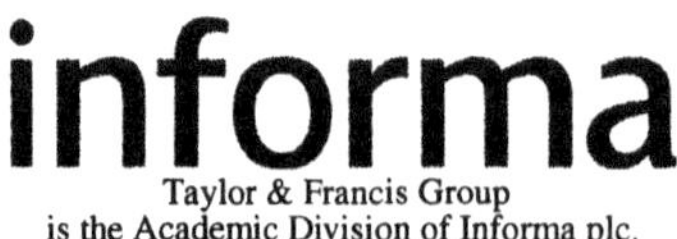

Visit the Taylor & Francis Web site at
http://www.taylorandfrancis.com

and the Routledge Web site at
http://www.routledge-ny.com

For Leo, the apple of my eye

Contents

List of Figures

Acknowledgments

In memory of Sherman Paul.

And with heartfelt thanks to:

Michael Cavanagh, my first and favorite poetry teacher; Michael Heller, for his encouragement early on; Virginia Jackson, who helped me bring this project to light; and to Prof. William Cain and Max Novick at Routledge, who recognized its merits. Much credit is due to my brothers, Christian and Paolo, and my parents, Colleen and Fernando, whose love and support have been liberal and unstinting. I am also grateful to fellow travelers Pam Brown, Lara Farina, and Michael Sohn, for years of commiseration. Finally, to my stalwart husband, Don Rauf, a world of love and thanks for seeing me through.

PERMISSIONS

Permission is acknowledged to reprint materials from the following sources:

"Discrete Series" by George Oppen, from *Collected Poems,* copyright 1934 by The Objectivist Press. Reprinted by permission of New Directions Publishing Corp. "Route" (excerpt) by George Oppen, from *Collected Poems,* copyright ©1968 by George Oppen. Reprinted by permission of New Directions Publishing Corp. "Blood from the Stone" (excerpt), "Of Being Numerous" (excerpt), and "World, World" (excerpt) by George Oppen, copyright ©1975 by George Oppen. Reprinted by permission of New Directions Publishing Corp. "Return" (excerpt) and "Time of the Missile" (excerpt) by George Oppen, from *New Collected Poems,* copyright ©1962 by George Oppen. Reprinted by permission of New Directions Publishing Corp. "Memory at 'The Modern'" (excerpt) by George Oppen, from *New Collected Poems,* copyright ©2000 by Linda Oppen. Reprinted by permission of New Directions Publishing Corp. "Monument" (excerpt) by George Oppen, from *New Collected Poems,* copyright ©2002 by Linda Oppen. Reprinted by permission of New Directions Publishing Corp.

All excerpts from George Oppen's correspondence from *The Selected Letters of George Oppen* ©Linda Oppen, quoted with permission. Reprinted by permission of Duke University Press and the Yale Collection of American Literature, Beinecke Rare Book Library.

Charles Reznikoff, *Testimony* (New York: Objectivist Press, 1934). Reprinted by permission of the Estate of Charles Reznikoff. *Rhythms II,* #8, "The Shoemaker" (#48 in *Fourth Group of Verse*), and *Jerusalem the Golden,* #69 from *The Poems of Charles Reznikoff, 1918–1975,* edited by Seamus Cooney (Boston: Black Sparrow Books, 2005). Reprinted by permission of Black Sparrow Books, an imprint of David R. Godine, Publisher, Boston.

Letter to Marie Sirkin dated 3 March 1930 from the *Selected Letters of Charles Reznikoff, 1917–1978,* edited by Milton Hindus (Santa Barbara: Black Sparrow Press, 1997). Reprinted by permission of the Estate of Charles Reznikoff.

"Down-Town," by William Carlos Williams, copyright ©1934 by the Estate of William Carlos Williams. Reprinted by permission of New Directions Publishing Corp. agents. "Brilliant Sad Sun" (excerpt), "Death" (excerpt), "Hemmed-in Males" (section 1), "Poem (As the cat)," "Rapid Transit" (excerpt), "The Attic Which Is Desire" (excerpt), "The Red Wheelbarrow," "The Sea Elephant" (excerpt), "To," and "Young Sycamore" by William Carlos Williams, from *Collected Poems 1909–1939,* VOLUME I, copyright ©1938 by New Directions Publishing Corp. Reprinted by permission of New Directions Publishing Corp.

"To Ezra Pound: 15 March 1933" (excerpt) and "To Louis Zukofsky: 18 July 1928" (excerpt) by William Carlos Williams, from *Selected Letters of William Carlos Williams,* copyright ©1957 by William Carlos Williams. Reprinted by permission of New Directions Publishing Corp.

"In a Station of the Metro" by Ezra Pound, from *Personae,* copyright ©1926 by Ezra Pound. Reprinted by permission of New Directions Publishing Corp.

"Pound to Zukofsky, 5 March 1928" by Ezra Pound, from *Pound/Zukofsky: Selected Letters of Ezra Pound and Louis Zukofsky,* copyright ©1981, 1987 by the Trustees of the Ezra Pound Literary Property Trust. Reprinted by permission of New Directions Publishing Corp.

Unpublished materials are from the following sources:

Carl Rakosi, excerpt from 5 July 1996 letter to the author from the Estate of Carl Rakosi by kind permission of Marilyn J. Kane.

Charles Reznikoff, working papers from the Mandeville Library of Special Collections, Courtesy the Estate of Charles Reznikoff.

Most of the images reprinted in this book are available to the public through the Prints and Photographs Division of the Library of Congress.

Lewis Wickes Hine, "Icarus High Up on Empire State (1931)" is reprinted with permission of the Photography Collection, Miriam and Ira D. Wallach Division of Art, Prints and Photographs, The New York Public Library, Astor, Lenox and Tilden Foundations.

Preface

A discrete series is a mathematical expression, signifying a "series of terms each of which is empirically derived, each of which is empirically true."[1] Like the successive glimpses of lit interiors one spies at night from a moving train, each particular in the series is related to the next, but no calculus can predict what the next one will be.

This study also qualifies as a discrete series. Situated within the larger narrative of the symbiosis between photography and modern poetry in America during the 1930s, each text I examine is a discrete object constituting a series of empirical statements, expressing certain empirical truths particular to its time and place. Charles Reznikoff's *Testimony,* George Oppen's *Discrete Series,* and William Carlos Williams *Collected Poems 1921–1931* were all issued in 1934 by the Objectivist Press, a short-lived publishing venture organized by a collective of like-minded writers that included Reznikoff, Oppen, and Williams as well as Ezra Pound and Louis Zukofsky. Reznikoff supplied the modest mission statement that was reproduced on the dust jackets: "The Objectivist Press is an organization of poets who are printing their own work and that of others they think ought to be printed."

Chapter 1 of this book locates the poetic origins of the American documentary movement and studies the emergence of Objectivist poetics within this documentary climate. Chapter 2 examines Reznikoff's *Testimony* and his transformation of legal case files into a new documentary form, the Objectivist prose poem. Chapter 3 concerns Oppen's masterful use of camera eye techniques in *Discrete Series* and his development of a unique documentary practice that would shape all of his subsequent writing. Chapter 4 explores the visual mechanisms at work in Williams's *Collected Poems 1921–1931* and investigates this text's relationship to the documentary imperatives of Objectivist poetics.

My larger enterprise in these pages has been to draw upon the evidence of historical documents in order to construct an image of the American past, circa 1934. I make use of documentary photographs and graphic images, correspondence and working papers, critical essays and reviews from large newspapers and little magazines, and transcripts of lectures and interviews dating from those years or reflecting back on them. Such a historical reconstruction will always reveal the biases of the writer. My particular biases determined my selection of materials for study as well as the oculocentric focus of this book. I have concentrated upon the construction and uses of visual images because of my own interests in this medium, but the 1930s should be remembered as a decade of the ear as much as of the eye.

Introduction

> The nineteenth century began by believing that what was reasonable was true and it would end up by believing that what it saw a photograph of was true.
>
> —William M. Ivans, Jr.

The 1930s in the United States were characterized by a national compulsion to record in detail, and thereby preserve, America's cultural life, which appeared threatened by economic collapse at home and the rise of fascism abroad. The period marked the first generalized awareness that something called "the American way of life" (the phrase came into currency during this decade) even existed, and that it deserved to be documented and preserved. This emerging national self-consciousness was expressed in various forms of documentary in written, aural, and visual media that constituted, according to historian Warren Susman, "the most overwhelming effort ever attempted to document in art, reportage, social science, and history the life and values of the American people."[1] As Paula Rabinowitz has noted, the age of documentation corresponded with the age of mechanical reproduction: New technologies of recording and transmission enabled words, sound, and images to be broadcast to mass audiences.[2] In the midst of this national ferment the camera emerged as the central documentary device, the medium that helped make America "real to itself."

The flourishing of documentary forms in the years between the wars was not strictly an American phenomenon, however. The term "documentary" was first used by the British film producer John Grierson in 1926, and documentary movements emerged in Canada, overseas in Europe, and in Russia that coincided with what was happening in the United States. The American variety was unique to the degree that it was sponsored by the U.S. federal government. For instance, in response to the economic crisis threatening rural Americans, the

Farm Security Administration hired a corps of photographers and sent them into the field, ostensibly to document the progress of FSA programs. Roy Stryker, head of the Photographic Unit of the FSA, recognized the broader significance of this effort and gave his photographers the freedom to document whatever caught their eye. Their collective efforts resulted in one of the most comprehensive records of American history ever assembled.

The American documentary movement was also distinguished from documentary efforts in other countries by virtue of its fundamentally poetic character; epitomized in the images of Walker Evans, this quality was widely recognized as the source of documentary photography's effectiveness—its power to stir feeling and incite change. In his introduction to the anthology *Proletarian Literature in the United States* (1935), Joseph Freeman saw the nation's renewed concern with "real things only" as issuing from a poetic source:

> The movement had its prophet in Walt Whitman, who broke with the "eternal values" of feudal literature and proclaimed the here and now; it focused its attention on New York, Chicago, San Francisco, Iowa, Alabama in the twentieth century.[3]

William Stott, in his book *Documentary Expression in Thirties America* (1973), also identifies Whitman as the patron saint of the American documentary movement: "[N]o other time so prized the Whitmanian 'I'—able to see, incorporate, and give voice to all human experience."[4] Yet that I/eye was oriented away from itself and toward others. Stott's book is an essential resource for any student of American documentary, and my enterprise here is much indebted to his extensive groundwork. Beyond Whitman, however, Stott makes only glancing references to documentary's influence on the poetry of the time; this leaves one to assume he subscribed to the long-standing view that most poetry in the thirties was either fatally out of touch with the ethos of the period or of historical interest purely as propaganda. Cary Nelson's important book *Repression and Recovery: Modern American Poetry and the Politics of Cultural Meaning 1910–1945* (1989) attempts to radically revise such assumptions about thirties poetry, as does the more recent critical anthology *Rewriting the Thirties: Modernism and After* (1997), edited by Keith Williams and Steven Matthews. Nonetheless, recent studies examining the transactions between photography and modern literature tend to focus almost exclusively on prose, and modern poetry is all but overlooked (see, for instance, Karen Jacobs's *The Eye's Mind: Literary Modernism and Visual Culture* [2001] and *Camera Works: Photography and the Twentieth-Century Word* by Michael North [2004]).

The continuing development of an indigenous American poetic tradition during the earlier part of the twentieth century was closely related to the nation's emerging cultural identity and the different means by which this national self-perception was expressed. Given the role that various forms of documentary expression played in the construction of a national identity, it seems hardly coincidental that the most historically important poetic movement of the 1930s should be based upon a documentary poetic. In a climate long considered hostile to literature, the thirties were nonetheless both formative and productive years for many of the poets associated with Objectivism, principally Louis Zukofsky, George Oppen, Charles Reznikoff, Lorine Niedecker, and Carl Rakosi—writers who comprise what French critic Serge Faucherau called "the first deliberately American movement in poetry."[5] During the thirties William Carlos Williams also associated closely with these poets, in particular with Zukofsky, his friend and editor for many years. For a time, the members of this group were in general agreement on a range of poetic matters, including the necessity of significant form as an antidote to a haphazard Imagism.

Rachel Blau DuPlessis offers a practical definition of the term *Objectivist,* a label that

> usefully designates a general aesthetic position in modern and contemporary poetry encompassing work based, generally, on "the real," on history not myth, on empiricism not projection, on the discrete not the unified, on vernacular prosodies and not traditional rhetoric, on "imagism," not "symbolism" or "surrealism," and on particulars with a dynamic relation to universals.[6]

Zukofsky's choice of this term to identify the qualities common to the writing he assembled in the "Objectivists" issue of *Poetry* magazine drew upon the vocabulary of optics to describe "The lens bringing the rays from an object to a focus." He further identified the features of this poetry as the "Desire for what is objectively perfect, inextricably the direction of historic and contemporary particulars."[7]

The notion of a documentary poetic that I formulate in this book draws on both of these statements. I hope, as well, to suggest some wider applications for the term "Objectivist" by situating it within the documentary currents of the time, particularly those related to social photography, a medium associated with "objectivity" and the disclosure of "truth." Contextualizing Reznikoff and Oppen within the frame of the documentary movement precludes them from being marginalized as obscure poets laboring at the fringes of American modernism. Instead, it shows how remarkably they anticipated and interpreted the aesthetic and ethical concerns of that period. A recognition of the documentary climate inhabited by these writers also illuminates the complex interrelations between their writing and their politics, which many scholars have regarded as ultimately at odds—the "political commitments they could not reconcile with their forms of literary attention," as Charles Altieri puts it.[8] An extended version of this project would necessarily include two other figures associated with the Objectivist group: Carl Rakosi, who referred to his *Americana* poems as "documentary on two levels,"[9] and Lorine Niedecker, whose poetic use of historical documents merits a study all to itself. In addition, Muriel Rukeyser's long serial poem *U.S. 1* (1938) deserves consideration in this context.

At a time when a majority of Americans distrusted what they read in the newspapers, many believed that seeing was believing, and that photographic evidence was equivalent to truth. The camera's growing preeminence as a documentary device was directly related to the status of the photographic image as a trace, a proof of "the real." Modern poetry and photography were intriguingly symbiotic forms of expression, and at no time in American history was this so apparent as during the 1930s. During these years, Reznikoff, Oppen, and Williams each constructed textual objects that aspired to the condition of the photograph.

Chapter One

The Poem in a Climate of Fact

Documentary: The creative treatment of actuality (John Grierson). The revelation of the truth through images (Paula Rabinowitz). (Use extended to poetry)—The obligation to present with exactitude the immanent qualities of the human condition and the reality of the world in which we find ourselves (Fred Thomas Sharp on the Objectivist poetic).

The "Objectivists" issue of *Poetry* magazine, guest-edited by Louis Zukofsky, appeared in February of 1931. Still a relatively unknown poet, Zukofsky had Ezra Pound to thank for this chance to introduce the venerable little magazine's readership to a new range of voices, poets Zukofsky believed shared his desire "to say things simply so that they will affect us as new again."[1] Editor Harriet Monroe's insistence that "You must have a movement" prompted Zukofsky's choice of "Objectivists," the provisional banner under which he assembled work by a cluster of his poetic contemporaries, including Charles Reznikoff and George Oppen. This issue of *Poetry* also includes Zukofsky's statements entitled "Program: 'Objectivists' 1931" and "Sincerity and Objectification." Here he delineates the parameters of a poetics based on "thinking with the things as they exist," exemplified in selected works by modernists such as Pound, William Carlos Williams, and Marianne Moore, but most particularly in the verses of Charles Reznikoff. With these notable exemptions, Zukofsky dismisses the labors of a decade of American poets, claiming that their work presents "neither consciousness of the 'objectively perfect' nor an interest in clear and vital 'particulars.' Nothing—neither a new object nor the stripping of an old to the light—was 'aimed at.'"[2]

OBJECTIVISTS AND IMAGISTS

In these critical statements Zukofsky insists upon a rigorous new criteria for poetry, one that owes much to the by-now-familiar tenets of Imagism outlined by F. S. Flint (though often attributed to Pound) in the pages of *Poetry* nearly twenty years earlier:

1. Direct treatment of the "thing" whether subjective or objective.

2. To use absolutely no word that does not contribute to the presentation.

3. As regarding rhythm: to compose in the sequence of the musical phrase, not in the sequence of the metronome.[3]

Also included in the March 1913 issue of *Poetry*—and originally intended as a rejection slip for contributors to the magazine—is Pound's statement "A Few Don'ts," which proposes a kind of "technical hygiene" (Hugh Kenner's phrase) for twentieth-century verse; in reaction against a "diluted Tennysonism," Pound proclaims that the new poetry will be "harder and saner . . . its force will lie in its truth," and it will distinguish itself by being "austere, direct, free from emotional slither."[4] Typically, Pound locates his exemplars in the distant (European) literary past, though the qualities he attributes to them seem strikingly modern: "In the art of Daniel and Cavalcanti, I have seen that precision which I miss in the Victorians, that explicit rendering, be it of external nature, or of emotion. Their testimony is of the eyewitness, their symptoms are first hand."[5] During the twenties, would-be Imagist poets with only a superficial grasp of Pound's ideas helped to expose Imagism's potential weakness: its tendency, in the wrong hands, to degenerate into a sloppy pictorialism. In his autobiography, William Carlos Williams offered this view of what the Objectivists aimed at correcting:

> The poem being an object (like a symphony or a cubist painting) it must be the purpose of the poet to make of his words a new form: to invent, that is, an object consonant with his day. This is what we wished to imply by Objectivism, an antidote, in a sense, to the bare image haphazardly presented in loose verse.[6]

Once the "antidote" of "Objectivism" had served its purpose (at least, as far as he was concerned), Williams was soon breaking camp to follow his own idiosyncratic compass.

SINCERITY AND OBJECTIFICATION

For Zukofsky there was no "Objectivism," only "Objectivists" and "objectification." To Pound's proscription that the Imagist poem must *present* rather than *re-present,* Zukofsky added the necessity of significant form, that is, form that is not imposed from without but intrinsic to the work. Beginning with its title, Zukofsky's "Sincerity and Objectification" specifies the two essential properties of the Objectivist poem: "sincerity," meaning "the care for detail," the accurate recording of particulars, and "objectification," meaning the realization of the intrinsic form of the poem: "tho it may not be harbored as solidity in the crook of an elbow, writing . . . which is an object or affects the mind as such."[7] In *A Homemade World,* Hugh Kenner's analogy for the relationship between the two terms is useful:

> Zukofsky's strategy was to plant a marker, "Sincerity," at a point the modern movement was widely understood to have reached, and then plant some distance away a second marker, "Objectification," to indicate a desirable direction of advance.[8]

Zukofsky's choice of "sincerity" as one of the poles with which he staked out the grounds for an Objectivist poetic merits examination, since the term attained a special currency during the thirties, and Zukofsky surely would have been sensitive to its connotations. For Wordsworth, sincerity meant being true to oneself, since he and other Romantic poets extolled individual experience (what Keats called "the egotistical sublime") as a means of achieving communion with God. Zukofsky's version of sincerity shifts the focus from the subject to the object and the relationship between the two; Objectivist sincerity is not about faithfulness to one's own emotion but rather to what is *out there,* to the "information," but this fidelity is also a test of the poet's own integrity. George Oppen put it this way: "that there is a moment, an actual time, when you believe something to be true, and you construct a meaning from these moments of conviction."[9] In *A Homemade World,* Kenner associates sincerity (Imagism's "direct treatment of the 'thing' whether subjective or objective") with Hemingway's notion of the "One True Sentence," a method for establishing a baseline of honesty in one's writing. While he dismissed Hemingway as an influence, Oppen echoed this idea when he told L. S. Dembo, "What I felt I was doing was beginning from imagism as a position of honesty. The first question at that time in poetry was simply the question of honesty, of sincerity."[10] Oppen remembers it as a palpable kind of pressure: "There seemed at the time a tremendous difficulty of honesty; the whole weight of sincerity seemed to rest on one's own shoulders."[11] In his influential essay "The Objectivist Tradition," Charles Altieri associates sincerity with a certain kind of artistic integrity that rejects dishonest or predetermined formal solutions: "Sincerity involves refusing the temptations of closure—both closure as a fixed form and closure as writing in the service of idea, doctrine, or abstract aesthetic ideal."[12]

In *They Must Be Represented: The Politics of Documentary,* Paula Rabinowitz notes that the dominant emotion of 1930s documentary was sincerity, shadowed by the danger of sentimentality.[13] The Objectivist version of sincerity as a directness of presentation, a shift of emphasis away from the subject-artist and toward the object, and a fidelity toward one's subject matter has much in common with the term as it was employed by documentary practitioners of the thirties and by interpreters of their work. In Objectivist poetics and documentary expression, sincerity has simultaneously a moral and an aesthetic value. In each case the term's connotations of authenticity and genuineness were associated with realness, a verifiable quality grounded in the immediate and the tangible. Sincerity was expressed in clean, "honest" lines, a clear focus, and the direct and detailed presentation associated with the aesthetics of "straight" photography; sentimentality, on the other hand, revealed itself aesthetically as redundancy, or the unessential comment or decoration. Cecelia Tichi's remark about Hemingway applies to Objectivist poetics in this respect: "[O]nly the artist who dares to expose himself in the efficient line can achieve the form of truth."[14]

Sincerity was also associated with "truth," a far more ineffable quality sustained, ultimately, by trust and faith. The mechanical nature of photography strengthened its claim to truth because its operations were largely automatic and therefore unsullied by human subjectivity. Still, the widespread public belief in the truth of documentary images depended upon acts of faith on the part of the viewer and the photographer: The viewer trusted the photographer not to falsify or manipulate the image, and the photographer trusted the viewer not to question her sincerity or her motives.[15] The attribution of sincerity offered the simultaneous assurance that something was both real and true—two essential components of documentary expression. The Objectivist poets, for their part, were concerned with form and with expressing sincerity formally in the creation of a poetic object by which various truths might be disclosed.

The term *objectification* describes a process (the making of an object) rather than a quality (*objective, objectivity*), but I suspect that Zukofsky chose the word in part because of these very associations. The quality of objectivity had been attributed to the photographic medium from the beginning (the root of the word signifies "lens" in at least four languages), a connection Zukofsky courted in his "Program: 'Objectivists' 1931" (see page 18 below). In the thirties, "objectivity" became part of the critical terminology that helped distinguish documentary photography from more "artistic" manifestations of the medium.

While signifying emotional detachment and neutrality, the word itself was not a neutral one; a journalist might be praised for his objective or unbiased reporting, but any claim to political objectivity was considered highly suspect in the "red thirties." Oppen insisted that the term did not mean objective in attitude but instead pointed to the poem's status as an object. Still, Objectivist poetry does avoid overt subjectivity, shunning the kind of ego focus that one associates with Romantic poetry or, later, with the so-called "confessional" poets such as Robert Lowell, Sylvia Plath, and W. D. Snodgrass. In both early and current studies of Objectivist poetry, commentators often remark on a characteristic neutrality of tone: Milton Hindus describes Reznikoff's style in *Testimony* as "cold on the surface"[16]; Alan Golding refers to the "neutrality of tone and presentation"[17] in Oppen's poems; and Ming-Qian Ma identifies moments in *Discrete Series* as "marked by what seems to be a clinical indifference,"[18] to cite only a few instances. The decision not to comment directly on what the poem presents amounts to a kind of bearing toward the Other, to what is out there, that relates to "objectivity" in the sense that it was applied to the documentary photography of the time. As the art critic Elizabeth McCausland wrote in her 1939 essay "Documentary Photography," "[W]e look at the world with a new orientation, more concerned with what is outside than with the inner ebb and flow of consciousness." Objectivist poetics reasserts, as does Pound's Imagism, the importance of the phenomenological world as a reference and validator for art at the same time that it insists upon a nonpredatory bearing toward that world.

RESPONSES AND FAILURES TO RESPOND

Harriet Monroe was sufficiently provoked by Zukofsky's editorial remarks in the Objectivist number of *Poetry* to publish, in the following issue, a counterattack entitled "The Arrogance of Youth." Here she describes how "With one grand annihilating gesture this young exponent of a 'new movement' sweeps off the earth the proud procession of poets whom, in our blindness and ignorance, we had fondly dedicated to immortality."[19] How it must have rankled Monroe to witness this upstart crow with the Groucho Marx eyebrows summarily dismissing all the poets she had nurtured in the pages of her magazine; nevertheless she manages to conclude with a show of good-natured indulgence: "If we cannot go all the way with Mr. Zukofsky and his February friends . . . we can at least cheer them on. They may be headed for a short life, but it should certainly be a merry one."[20]

Notwithstanding Monroe's incapacity to take the measure of these poets, what Altieri calls the "Objectivist tradition" has proven longer lived than Imagism, from which it adapted its theoretical foundations. Zukofsky, Oppen, Reznikoff, and Rakosi (along with Lorine Niedecker, whose work did not appear in this issue of *Poetry*) all continue to be subjects of refocused critical attention, and successive generations of contemporary poets (notably Jack Spicer, Rae Armantrout, Charles Bernstein and the Language poets) continue to rediscover and to learn from these writers. In contrast, the reputations of poets such as Robinson Jeffers, Edna St. Vincent Millay, Amy Lowell, and Elinor Wylie, all championed by Monroe, have dwindled in the intervening years.

The February 1931 issue of *Poetry* represents a seminal text in the history of Objectivist poetics. Yet at the time of its publication only an isolated few were alert to its significances. Niedecker, who discovered here a gathering of writers whose work was congenial to her own, recognized a poetic ally in Zukofsky, and initiated a correspondence with him that would last for forty years. Another subscriber returned his copy, canceling his subscription and demanding a refund. Zukofsky's impatience at the general lack of response to his poetic salvo was evident six months later when he spoke at the Gotham Book Mart in New York City: "The 'objectivists' number of Poetry appeared in February. Since then there have been March, April, May, June, July and we are now past the middle of August. Don't write, telegraph."[21]

After the 1929 stock market crash, concerns over the state of American poetry must have struck many as increasingly beside the point. By February of 1931, seven million Americans were already out of work; two years later, this number would increase to one in four.[22] *The New York Times* was preoccupied with the closure of the Bank of the United States and the management of drought relief; reports of murder/suicides prompted by financial loss were appearing in the newspapers.[23] The pressures of "reality" were claiming precedence, and all forms of fiction would come to seem insufficiently serious responses to the crises of the day.[24]

A majority of Americans has always viewed poetry with hostile indifference, but even those who cared deeply about literature marked the change in climate during the thirties. Lisa Steinman writes that "American literary critics had accepted the modern idea that poetry should be part of the real world—and they faulted Wallace Stevens' first two volumes [*Harmonium* 1923; *Ideas of Order* 1935] for their distance from the harsh reality of the Depression."[25] In a letter to Ronald Lane Latimer postmarked October 1935, Stevens acknowledged: " . . . [W]e live in a different time, and life means a good deal more to us now-a-days than literature does."[26] Money earmarked for new literary ventures could be better spent feeding the hungry.[27] In *Axel's Castle* (1931), Edmund Wilson ruefully remarks that "for some reason or other, verse as a technique of literary expression is being abandoned by humanity altogether."[28]

On the Left, where intellectuals allied themselves in growing numbers during these years, the prevailing ideology dictated that poets should contribute to the class struggle. In 1935, addressing the first American Writers' Congress, Isidor Schneider detailed the functions of poetry in a revolutionary society:

> [A]s a social art poetry has a specially hopeful future in a socialized state. Its capacity for sonorous, memorable, and ceremonious utterance will make it useful. It will have a new set of universal values to deal with, a whole new history to digest, a new ethics to promote, a new range of aesthetics in nature and humanity, a new pantheon of heroes to enshrine.[29]

In his unfavorable review of *Testimony* and *Jerusalem the Golden*, Herman Spector blasted Reznikoff for his apparent political detachment:

> Profound world events cannot leave a poet of his integrity and sanguine temperament cynical or indifferent. He must soon realize that history permits him the alternative: either to succumb to the paralysis of reaction, or else to take that great leap forward which is the way of revolution. Impartiality is a myth which defeatists take with them into oblivion.[30]

Poets such as Zukofsky and Oppen who were, during this period, politically committed Marxists (George and Mary Oppen joined the Communist Party in 1935; Zukofsky worked on the party's behalf, though he never became an official member), were also expected to take sides. The radical left believed that the poet could contribute to the revolution, as long as he toed the party line. However, the general feeling was that verse was too frivolous a medium to address the exigencies of the present time. People were impatient with an art that supposedly concerned itself with private matters in the midst of a social cataclysm and believed that poets should address themselves to realities, social concerns, and the "surface drama" (Kazin) of the times.

PUBLISHING VENTURES AND POETIC SILENCES

Though this "climate of fact" was supposedly inimical to poetry, these were nevertheless productive years for many of the writers associated with Objectivism. The February 1931 issue of *Poetry* magazine was followed in 1932 by *An "Objectivists" Anthology*, also edited by Zukofsky, which included work by

Oppen, Rakosi, and Reznikoff, as well by Pound, Williams, and T. S. Eliot ("Marina"). Two joint publishing ventures—TO Publishers and the Objectivist Press—enabled Zukofsky and Oppen to issue their own poetry as well as work by Reznikoff and Williams. Between 1929 and 1941 Reznikoff published five collections of verse as well as an early version of *Testimony* and two novels. Rakosi's *Selected Poems* was issued by New Directions in 1941. Niedecker's writing from the period appeared in a few magazines and journals, although her first volume of verse came after the war (*New Goose,* 1946).

This productivity seems all the more remarkable when one considers that most of this work was accomplished in the first few years of the decade, for the thirties also marked the beginning of extended periods of poetic silence for Reznikoff, Oppen, and Rakosi. After *Going To and Fro and Walking Up and Down* came out in 1941, Reznikoff did not produce another volume of poems for eighteen years. *Discrete Series* appeared in 1934, and Oppen would not publish again until *The Materials* in 1962, choosing instead to direct his energies into political activism. Similarly, Rakosi's commitment to politics occasioned a withdrawal from poetic production that lasted from the mid-thirties until the sixties. As Rakosi told L. S. Dembo,

> I took very literally the basic Marxian ideas about literature having to be an instrument for social change, for expressing the needs and desires of large masses of people. And believing that, I couldn't write poetry, because the poetry that I could write could not achieve those ends.[31]

Oppen attributed his own poetic silence to his incapacity to regard literature of any kind as an effective and practical response to the suffering he witnessed during those years. It would not have been honest, Oppen said, to pretend that by writing political poetry one could improve social conditions.[32]

THE DOCUMENTARY CLIMATE

Despite the demands of the time and the claims of political activism, these poets nonetheless managed to produce a body of work that continues to be read and written about and discussed today, a poetry as expressive of a certain historical moment as the documentary photography that proliferated later in the decade. Zukofsky, Reznikoff, Oppen, Niedecker, and Rakosi all formulated their poetics within an emerging documentary climate that would impact nearly every aspect of American culture during the 1930s. While the term "documentary photography" did not come into popular use until the end of this period, the currents that necessitated its invention had long permeated American culture. In *Documentary Expression and Thirties America,* William Stott locates a documentary motive at work in everything from the literature, theater, and dance to the education and the social sciences of this decade.[33]

The thirties also marked a rare moment in American history when artists and the general public experienced a sense of national solidarity in response to current events, a unity encouraged by government policies that funded the arts as public works. Recalling those days, Rakosi insisted that "[D]espite the very hard times, there was an explosion of optimism and affirmative energy. Everything seemed possible."[34] In *Exile's Return,* Malcolm Cowley also mentions the

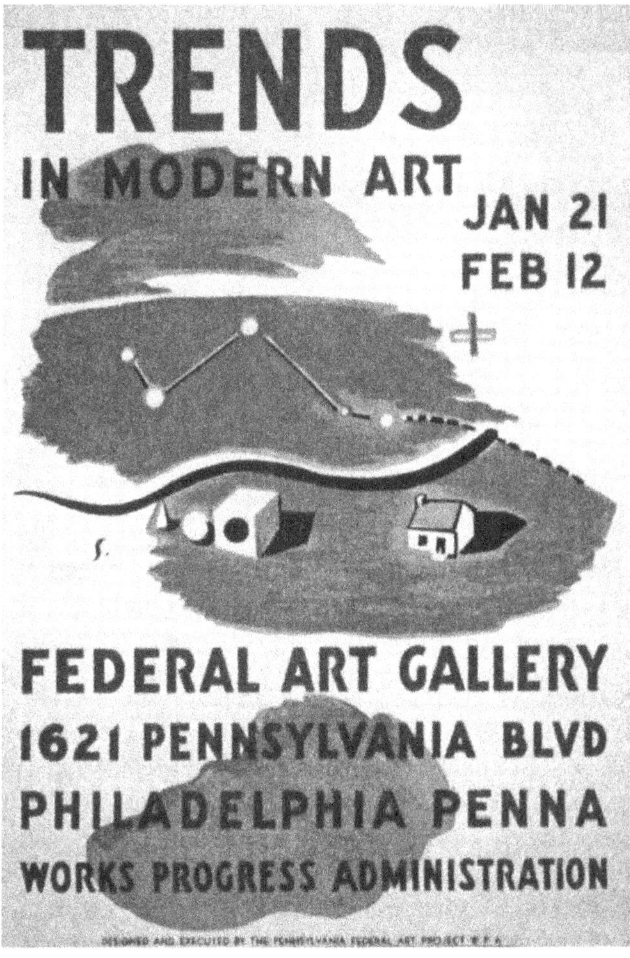

Fig. 1.1 WPA poster, Trends in Modern Art (1935–1939)
Library of Congress, Prints and Photographs Division, LC-USZC2-901

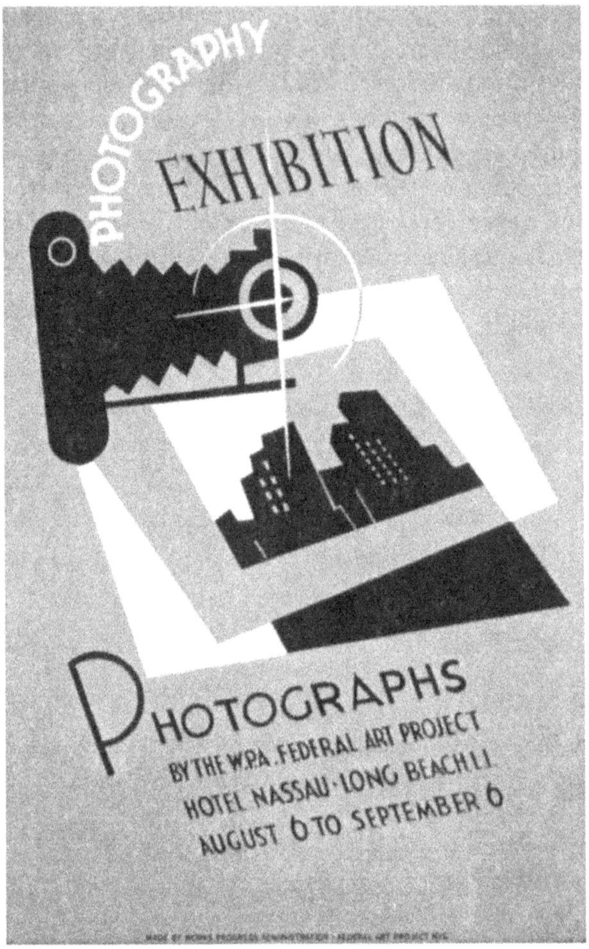

Fig. 1.2 WPA poster, Federal Art Project, Photography Exhibition (1941)
Library of Congress, Prints and Photographs Division, LC-USZC2-927

strange excitement of the time: "[T]he years 1933 and 1934 were a madly hopeful time when it seemed that great changes in the economic system were already under way."[35] The Works Progress Administration (WPA) and other federally funded programs were launched during the Depression in order to create jobs for writers and artists; their contributions to the national culture helped to introduce the public to a rich variety of art (see figures 1.1 and 1.2) and to move the artist in from the margins of society toward the center. At no time before or since have writers and artists in the United States enjoyed such governmental patronage without being subject to certain restrictions or outright censorship; the trend today is toward increasing constraints. According to Stott, however, while "[t]he WPA artists were free to do what they wanted, . . . all they wanted to do was document America."[36] Because of these jobs, many writers were able to sustain themselves and their families during the Depression. Zukofsky and Niedecker were both employed by the WPA during this period: Between 1934 and 1942 Zukofsky contributed to a series of WPA projects including the superb Index of American Design, and Niedecker helped research and write the Wisconsin State Guide, part of the massive documentary effort that resulted in the American Guide Series.

Given the documentary ethos of the times, the Objectivist poets were doubtless influenced by this increasingly ubiquitous genre, though the disparities in their temperaments and methods obviously resulted in differing expressions of that influence. As I argue in the following chapters, Objectivist poetry between the world wars had more in common with documentary images and the particular stance toward "the real" that these images embodied than with much of the poetry written in the United States during the same period. This convergence of two very different art forms seems all the more remarkable when one considers that the literary evidence anticipates much of the documentary evidence, though not the ideological currents that produced it.

CAPTURING THE ACTUAL

The notion, widespread during the 1930s, that imaginative works are somehow inadequate or irrelevant to the presentation of actualities was, in fact, a relatively new phenomenon. During the nineteenth and early twentieth centuries, fiction provided an important source of information about actuality,[37] which continues to influence how we imagine certain historical periods today. When we think of the 1920s, for instance, our impressions of that decade—the particular images we have of how people dressed and spoke and behaved—are derived largely from fictional sources: the novels of F. Scott Fitzgerald and Ernest Hemingway, perhaps, or from contemporary films based on those sources. Even individuals with no direct experience of the original works will be influenced by the fund of historical information these texts embody and continue to disseminate.

In contrast, our national memory of the years between the world wars is based largely on nonfiction documents, especially on the photographic record of the time. Specific images will come readily to mind: people standing in a breadline, the shabby rooms of a sharecropper's shack, the long-suffering face of Dorothea Lange's iconic "Migrant Mother" (an image recently used to advertise public television programming). The literary texts we associate with this period—Steinbeck's *The Grapes of Wrath* (1939), Dos Passos's U.S.A. Trilogy (1938), and Evans and Agee's *Let Us Now Praise Famous Men* (1941), for instance—are all hybrids, notable for the ways in which they all incorporate materials and techniques to evoke a documentary style. The Depression years bring to mind such specific images, even for those born decades later, because the visual evidence of what took place in small towns and cities across the country was made a matter of record, and people looked to these records, rather than to fictional sources, for information about the times in which they lived. Furthermore, this information was available to people who couldn't (or wouldn't) read. Even the gray tones of black-and-white photography seem suited to the prevailing mood of those years. At a time when public confidence in the print media had plummeted,[38] photographic images could still, it seemed, be trusted to show people the truth.

Unlike representational or even photorealistic painting, photography works by light, which leaves evidence of itself in the emulsion of the film or photographic plate. (Even digital photography begins with light, before translating it into pixels.) Thus, "photography was thought to permit nature to be the means and agency of its own representation."[39] Metaphors describing early photographs, such as "the pencil of nature," underscore this idea, figuring nature itself as the artist/creator. The art historian Rosalind Krauss categorizes the photograph as an index or a trace, which she defines as "a signifying mark that bears a connection to the thing it represents by having been caused, physically, by its referent."[40] In other words, a photograph is proof that such a thing as external reality exists. The photographic image constitutes a record of the existence of a particular subject and the evidence of a claim to having been in its presence, endowing photography with a status with regard to the real that is not shared by any other visual medium.

Photographic technology imitates human physiology at the same time that it extends it: The camera "sees" like an eye (that is, an aperture opens to admit rays of light, which are registered by the mechanism), and even appropriates a name from that organ for its central component: the lens. Indeed, the distinction between our own perception and the objectified record of the photographer's seeing can become blurred, so that the sight of a photograph (even a black-and-white image) may be confused, years later, with an actual memory of an event; looking at family pictures can generate a new, belated "memory" of one's childhood. This is no less true culturally than it is individually. In the aftermath of the 1929 stock market crash and before the United States entered the Second World War, photographic images documenting the particulars of "the American experience" had become a ubiquitous feature of that experience. These images—transmitted first via newsreels and the proliferating medium of photo magazines such as *Life* and *Look* and later through documentary books such as Erskine Caldwell and Margaret Bourke-White's *You Have Seen Their Faces* (1937) and Dorothea Lange and Paul Taylor's *American Exodus* (1939)—served both to verify and to vivify Americans' own experiences of these years. Such images helped construct, in immeasurable ways, Americans' sense of their own national history and cultural life.

True, much of the documentary photography produced between the wars served to reveal and underscore an economic imbalance, exposing the conditions of dispossessed and impoverished (usually rural) Americans to the inspection of the middle-class viewer (usually urban) who could consume such images in relative comfort. But the poor also consume images, as Walker Evans's interior studies so frequently remind us (see figure 1.3). Scenes people witnessed on the streets of their own towns—failing businesses and forced evictions, but also the rites and customs of their communities—were replayed in darkened theaters and on the pages of magazines, confirming their own experiences, exposing them to new experiences, and imbuing everything with a new—an altered—significance.

After looking at the photographs in an old family album, a child I know concluded quite reasonably that reality itself prior to about 1965 came exclusively in black and white. Counterintuitive as it may seem, black-and-white photography still conveys a certain veracity for which it is difficult to fully account. For this reason, documentary photography's commitment to making a record of the actual did not often extend to the regular use of color film, though the technology was available as early as 1907. Farm Security Administration (FSA) photographers produced both black-and-white and color images in the course of their work, but the former are the ones we remember and which have since attained an iconic status. Orson Welles's 1941 film *Citizen Kane* remarks on the fact that even though life happens in color, black-and-white film looks more "realistic," more authentic. In *Camera Lucida,* Roland Barthes maintains that the black-and-white image is more true, and that the addition of color actually interferes with the transfer of light from the original photographic subject to the observer.[41] Clearly, photography's claim to truth has as much to do with aesthetics and the style of realism we were raised on as with the medium's supposed relationship to reality.

"[P]hotography is not an art in the old sense," wrote Elizabeth McCausland in 1939. "It is not a romantic, impressionistic medium, dependent on subjective factors and ignoring the objective. It is bound to realism in as complex a way as buildings are bound to the earth by the pull of gravitation. . . ."[42] In today's world of digitized images, which can be altered to create whatever version of "reality" one desires, we are witnessing the final

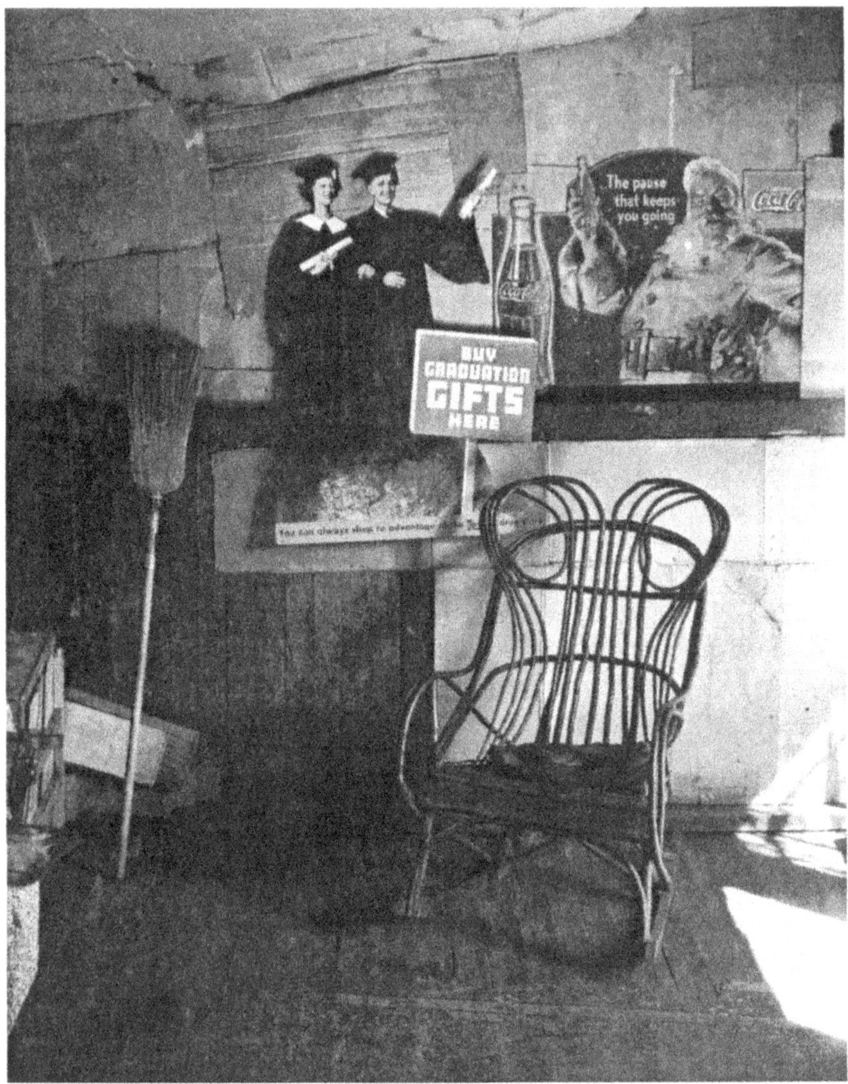

Fig. 1.3 Walker Evans. Scott's Run mining camps near Morgantown, West Virginia. Domestic interior. Shack at Osage (1935). Library of Congress, Prints and Photographs Division, LC-USF342-TO1-000895-A DLC

dismantling of the association between photography and truth that people largely subscribed to during the previous century. It's not that people in the past were too naïve to appreciate that the camera can lie; even at the time, in

Stalinist Russia, party members who had fallen out of favor were excised from official photographs, erasures that coincided with their actual disappearance into gulags and unmarked mass graves.[43] However, people generally agreed that the camera should not be used to falsify reality but to record and present it, and they trusted documentary photographers' commitment to these objectives.

WALKER EVANS AND THE POETRY OF THE LENS

As documentary photography gained recognition as an artistic medium in its own right—an achievement that culminated, in 1938, in Walker Evans's show entitled "American Photographs" at the Museum of Modern Art in New York[44]—critics praised documentary images for their "lyricism" and "poetic" qualities. In his afterward accompanying the book of the show, Lincoln Kirstein, editor of the literary quarterly *Hound & Horn,* places Evans in the company of writers when he declares that "[his] eye is a poet's eye. It finds corroboration in the poet's voice."[45] Even before the MOMA show, Evans's photographs (portraits of writers such as Hart Crane but also images of homeless men sleeping in the doorways of lower Manhattan) were often published in *Hound & Horn,* demonstrating Kirstein's belief in their artistic and specifically in their literary merit. Maria Morris Hambourg, a curator of photographs at the Metropolitan Museum of Art, called Evans "the poet laureate of the documentary style."[46] Evans's view of his own work derived emphatically from literary sources; he had first hoped to be a fiction writer, and he persisted in referring to himself as "a man of literature." When questioned about his influences, Evans cited Baudelaire ("in spirit"), Henry James, Hemingway, Joyce, and Gustave Flaubert.

> I incorporated Flaubert's method . . . in two ways; both his realism, or naturalism, and his objectivity of treatment. The non-appearance of the author. The non-subjectivity. That is literally applicable to the way I want to use a camera and do.[47]

Flaubert's detailed and exact presentation of bourgeois life has obvious analogies to Evans's calmly attentive mechanical gaze. More than that of any other writer, Flaubert's example demonstrated to Evans that art could adopt a documentary style without relinquishing form. In this study I concentrate principally on the documentary photography of Walker Evans, to the exclusion of many other photographers working at that time, because he represents a bridge between the photography and the literature of the 1930s and thus a useful means of exploring the relationship between these two arts. Other photographers contemporary to Evans, notably Berenice Abbott and Ben Shahn, were working in a similar vein. However, an examination of Evans's photographic influences reveals the presence of an American documentary tradition with strong literary affiliations beginning with the work of Mathew Brady.[48] Here is Walker Evans lecturing at Yale University on the subject of "Lyrical Documentary":

> [W]hat I believe is really good in the so-called documentary approach in photography is the addition of lyricism. Further, that the lyric is usually produced unconsciously and even unintentionally and accidentally by the cameraman—. . . The real thing that I'm talking about has purity and a certain severity, rigor, simplicity, directness, clarity, and it is without artistic pretension in a self-conscious sense of the word.[49]

The nature of Evans's images and his photographic ambitions invite comparisons with the poetics of George Oppen and William Carlos Williams, which anticipated much of Evans's work during the thirties. Many of Evans's artistic concerns ("deconstruction of the photographic portrait; the use of the random as a creative principal; reflections on the appropriation of the consumer image; seriality . . . in the photographic process; the role of the vernacular object . . . ; the ambiguity in photography of art and document . . . and the question of anonymity . . . the aesthetic of the real"[50]) have correlations in the work of these poets, which I examine in chapters 3 and 4 of this book. Finally, Evans's singular interpretation of what constitutes a "documentary style" helps illuminate the kind of documentary motive I locate in the early work of these poets and may help to clarify aspects of their writing that have troubled commentators over the years.

LYRICAL VALUES

Walker Evans was certainly not the only documentary photographer whose images prompted comparisons to literature. Poetic terms and analogies crop up frequently in the critical vocabulary applied to documentary images, both in the United States and in Europe. John Grierson, the British producer and critic who originated the term *documentary,* described Robert Flaherty's documentary film *Moana* (1926) as "a poetic record of Polynesian tribal life."[51] Later, Grierson wrote that documentary "has given itself the job of making poetry where no poet has gone before it."[52] Critics in France were particularly concerned with lyrical values. In his tribute to the late Eugene Atget

(1856–1927), the Surrealist poet Robert Desnos describes Atget's work as belonging to the "lyrical documentary vein" of photography: "But what documents! For thirty years, Atget has photographed all of Paris with the marvelous objective of creating a dream and a surprise. These are . . . the visions of a poet, bequeathed to poets."[53] Pierre Mac Orlan, a French poet and critic of photography, wrote in a 1928 essay that documentary photography is "literary without knowing it, because it is no more than a document of contemporary life captured at the right moment by an author capable of grasping that moment."[54] Mac Orlan also unifies the two art forms in a single practitioner when he refers to "photographer-poets like Man Ray and [André] Kertesz."[55] As late as 1946, James Agee was praising the "lyrical photographs" of Helen Levitt in the essay he wrote to accompany her book, *A Way of Seeing*. And in the review of a 1998 retrospective of Evans's photographs in New York City, the headline in the *New York Times* read: "Walker Evans Found the Poetry in Life's Unvarnished Details."[56] So, despite the tendency to dismiss poetry's relevance to the times, the term itself apparently retained (and still retains) its currency as a label signifying a particular kind of value in documentary photography.

WRITING WITH LIGHT

It may seem strange that such fundamentally emotional terms of approbation would be so consistently applied to documentary photography, that supposedly objective medium for recording reality, an operation accomplished mostly by machine. The persistent linking of photography and literature—specifically the values of lyric poetry—in the critical commentary of the times suggests that an essential affinity exists between these arts. The etymology of the word *photography* points to literature, since it literally means "writing with light." Walker Evans called photography "the most literary of the graphic arts."[57] An image is a kind of writing, as Alan Trachtenberg points out. Further, he notes that "photographs [are] the most written upon, under, above, and around of all visual artifacts."[58] Documentary photographs, in particular, depend for their principal effects on captions that identify the subjects pictured and the times and places the photographs were taken. (See chapter 2 of this book for examples of the detailed captions that accompanied Lewis Hine's images.) Roy Stryker, head of the Photographic Unit of the Farm Security Administration (FSA), acknowledged the reliance of documentary images on written text when he said, "The photograph is only the subsidiary, the little brother, of the word. . . . In truth there's only one picture in a hundred thousand that can stand alone as a piece of communication."[59]

Despite Stryker's contention that the photographic image was subordinate to the word, many observers recognized that photography represented an important link between the artistic avant-garde and an evolving mass technological culture. The camera was mass-produced and shared in the precision and economy of machine processes. Poets were influenced by the camera as an idea and excited by the possibilities the medium presented, but photographers also chose to align themselves with new literary developments, resulting in a great deal of cross-pollination between the two arts.

THE IMAGE

By 1931, when Zukofsky's "Objectivists" issue of *Poetry* appeared, an entire discourse was already established in the critical writings of influential European artists such as Man Ray and László Moholy-Nagy, much of it in agreement with Salvador Dali's contention that "photographic testimony . . . is always and ESSENTIALLY THE SUREST VEHICLE OF POETRY."[60] As Susan Sontag would observe nearly a half century later, "the ethos of photography, that of schooling us in 'intensive seeing' . . . seems closer to that of modernist poetry than that of painting."[61] With this in mind, then, it is worth noting that Zukofsky's "Program: 'Objectivists' 1931" begins with an image pertaining to photography:

> *An Objective: (Optics)—The lens bringing the rays from an object to a focus. (Military use)—That which is aimed at. (Use extended to poetry)—Desire for what is objectively perfect, inextricably the direction of historic and contemporary particulars.*

Zukofsky's lexicon functions as a lens, too, focusing various meanings, both stated and implied: *Merriam-Webster's Dictionary* defines *objective* as "a lens or system of lenses that forms an image of an object." In French, *objectif* means lens; in Spanish, *objectivo;* in German, *Objektiv.* Zukofsky's assertion that the poet's job is, as Fred Thomas Sharp writes, "to present with exactitude the immanent qualities of the human condition and the reality of the world in which we find ourselves"[62] amounts to a statement of documentary intention; Zukofsky's definition of "an Objective" as "the rays of an object brought to a focus" exposes certain affinities between his poetic aims and the photographic process.

This study explores aspects of the relationship between the documentary photographic image and the Objectivist poetic image. The Objectivists derived their notion of the image from Imagism, although Oppen in particular found Pound's version of the image (i.e., the Image) problematic and took pains to distinguish his own sense of it from Pound's. In 1913, in the pages of *Poetry* magazine, Pound had defined the Image as "that which presents an intellectual and emotional complex in an instant of time."[63] Based on this definition and later elaborations of Pound's poetics, it would be an error to interpret this word in strictly visual terms; this was one mistake that led to the degenerated version of Imagism that Pound derided as "Amygism," after Amy Lowell. However, nothing in Pound's definition precludes a visual interpretation, either. When Herbert Schneidau writes that Pound was after not "pictures in verse" but something with the same "hard-edged quality, the sharp definition, that the visual scene furnishes,"[64] it is hard not to think of a photograph. Schneidau resorts to such an analogy when he describes how Pound's Image instantaneously presents "an intellectual and emotional complex" "as a photograph might try to capture in a chance gesture or unguarded expression some revelation of mood or personality traceable to a set of fixed ideas."[65] A successful Image has the same effect on us as a successful photograph: In the exactness of its presentation the singular quality of its subject, its essence (its truth?), shines through.

In his famous essay "Meditations on a Hobby horse," the art historian E. H. Gombrich identifies the hobby horse as constituting what he calls "a conceptual image." The hobby horse is not mimetic; it does not attempt to duplicate an actual horse—it may be simply a stick "body" with a potato "head" impaled on one end. The hobby horse is an autonomous object in the world, but its meaning and use depends upon the existence of real horses.[66] Pound's Image and that of the Objectivist poets has a comparable relationship to the "actual world" in that it hovers between autonomy and referentiality in the same sense that Gombrich's hobby horse does. To the extent that it testifies to the existence of the actual world (Oppen: "that there is something to stand on"), the Objectivist image, like a photograph, qualifies as an index or trace. A desire to attend to a reality independent from, and antecedent to, the poem itself led to the Objectivists' version of the image "as a factor of a realistic art, a realist art in that the poem is concerned with a fact it did not create,"[67] as Oppen wrote.

Photographic images reproduce the ability of the human eye to select and focus. Their power depends, in part, upon an assumption that simply by seeing we may come to know and understand the world around us. Thus, most forms of documentary expression situate the eye as the principal agency of relation. The poets I am concerned with in this study frankly privileged the visual in their work and regarded vision as the preeminent poetic faculty. Pound's choice of the word *image,* and the Objectivist poets' adoption of this term, demonstrate their willingness to acknowledge a correlation between the poetic image and other kinds of images. Granted, the word *image* historically has been a slippery one, encompassing things as diverse as a painting to a vivid figure of speech to a picture that floats before the mind's eye to the publicly held perception of a politician, and Pound's version of the term is similarly inclusive. The documentary photographer Ben Shahn was not concerned with making distinctions: "To me images are images. I don't care whether they're made with pen, pencil, brush, they're images, and they can be moving or not."[68] According to Gombrich, "all art is image-making."[69]

DOCUMENTARY ART

Alan Golding, in his essay entitled "Politics and Style in Oppen's *Discrete Series,*" discusses the importance of this work "as both a social and poetic document—a document of what one thoughtful leftist poet felt it important to consider in the 1930s."[70] When *Discrete Series* was published in 1934, the categories of "document" and "artwork" were by no means mutually exclusive. Modernism was still busy questioning such distinctions: In poetry, one finds Eliot's fragments shoring up the ruins in *The Waste Land* (1922); Pound was incorporating prose documents in his Malatesta Cantos, as would Williams in *Paterson,* roughly fifty percent of which is quotations. Zukofsky's "A" registered other voices and sounds like a radio telescope. Prose texts featuring quotation include James Joyce's *Ulysses* and Virginia Woolf's *To the Lighthouse.* Earlier in the century, Cubist collages included ticket stubs and other effluvia from daily life in order to interrogate the concept of the "art object." The introduction of found objects from the "real" world calls attention to the constructedness of "reality" in the same way that incorporating quotations and pieces of documents alerts us to language as an object of representation rather than as a means of representation.[71]

This intentional testing and subversion of the categories of document and artwork brought about changes in public perceptions of art that influenced thinking about photography, too. A photograph could be both a work of art and a document and might, in fact, benefit from partaking in the status of each. In an author's note following her documentary poem *The Book of the Dead* (in *U.S. 1,* 1938), Muriel Rukeyser wrote, "Local images have one kind of reality. U.S. 1 will, I hope, have that kind and another too. Poetry can extend the document."[72] For a document to be regarded as art it must transcend its function as mere evidence and convey a larger, universal truth. On the other hand, when an artwork is seen as a document it becomes historical, expressive of its particular time and seen as embedded in and constituted by a web of social and political relationships. The French critic Florent

Fels insisted that "[a] good photograph is, above all, a good document."[73] Photography was a new medium, with no real history or established traditions; because of its unprecedented relationship to "reality," photography forced a redefinition of the critical vocabulary pertaining to the visual arts. Despite the groundwork of modernism, commentators have been troubled by the essential ambiguity in photography regarding the status of the image as art or document, as have many photographer/artists themselves. As is the case with "image," the term "document" is problematic. Walker Evans, one of the first photographers to have his images displayed on the walls of a major museum, grappled with this term: "Documentary? That's a very sophisticated and misleading word. . . . You have to have a sophisticated ear to receive that word."[74] Evans finally settled on "documentary style" to characterize his camera work, which seeks to reconcile the aesthetic and the documentary aspects of his pictures in a single phrase.

ORIGINS OF A DOCUMENTARY MOTIVE IN AMERICAN POETRY

> It is difficult to say whether Walker Evans created the vocabulary, grammar, and ethics of seeing that still shape our vision of the cultural landscape of 1930s America or whether the near perfection of his vision simply confirmed sentiments that had been in the air since Walt Whitman urged Americans to sing the praises of everyday life in the United States. (Timothy Davis in *Mapping American Culture*)[75]

The origins of the documentary style that we associate with so many aspects of the thirties can be traced back to an older period in American history. As early as 1855, Walt Whitman was praising a shift toward "the real" that would characterize so many of the principal aesthetic, philosophical, scientific, technological, and political movements of the twentieth century. Whitman's conviction that

> the true use for the imaginative faculty of modern times is to give ultimate vivification to facts, to science, and to common lives, endowing them with the glows and glories and final illustriousness which belong to every real thing, and to real things only[76]

describes a kind of documentary function that Whitman clearly regarded as essential to the development of a distinctively American poetry. The influential photography critic Beaumont Newhall incorporated Whitman's words into his definition of documentary, when he characterized it as "an approach which makes use of the artistic faculties to give 'vivification to fact.'"[77] For Whitman, who conceived of the poetic as inseparable from the political, establishing a national poetic tradition was a means to—and an embodiment of—the cohesion of the nation itself. As he states in his 1855 preface to *Leaves of Grass*, Whitman regarded "the United States as the greatest poem."[78] Whitman recognized the uniqueness of the American democracy and believed, after Emerson, that the United States demanded both a poet and a poetic as unprecedented as the nation itself to articulate in verse such a bold social experiment. Whitman insisted that the poet's eye must look outward toward the phenomenal world; his conviction that the imaginative powers of art

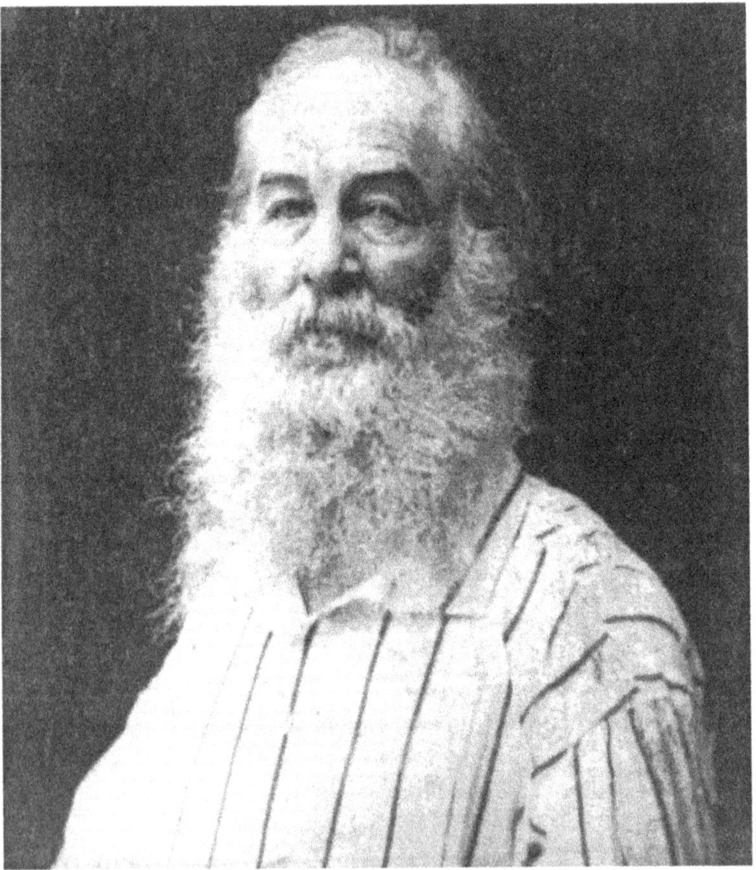

Fig. 1.4 Mathew Brady. Portrait of Walt Whitman (1888?)
Library of Congress, Prints and Photographs Division, LC-USZ62-89957

should be directed to work exclusively upon real things reveals the documentary basis of the new poetry that Whitman saw issuing from America.

While Whitman was busy in Brooklyn shaping the poetic future of the nation, Mathew Brady was pursuing another documentary project at his studio on Broadway in Manhattan, photographing eminent contemporaries for his Gallery of Illustrious Americans, and making a name for himself even before he produced his famous images of the Civil War. Whitman and Brady knew each other and they discussed history and photography on many occasions,[79] so it seems fair to say that American poetry and documentary photography developed in each other's company. Alan Trachtenberg has noted how much Whitman enjoyed being photographed; he frequently sat for portraits at Brady's studio (see figure 1.4) and included updated images of himself in successive editions of *Leaves of Grass.*[80]

BRADY'S LITERARY APPROACH TO THE IMAGE

During the 1930s, Brady's extraordinary camera work was brought back before the public's eye when a selection of Civil War images produced by Brady's studio (actually a group of photographers working under this trademark) appeared in the literary journal *Hound & Horn* in 1933 (see figures 1.5 and 1.6). In his book published the following year, George Oppen included a poem showing how the presentness of the past is objectified, detailing the very particulars that can be seen in Brady's images:

> Civil war photo:
> Grass near the lens;
> Man in the field
> In silk hat. Daylight.
> The cannon of that day
> In our parks.
> (from *Discrete Series, NCP,* 21)

An essay by Charles Flato that accompanies the images in *Hound & Horn* describes Brady's approach as literary in the manner in which

> he placed object against contrasting object, idea as opposed to idea, in closer proximity than a less literary-minded artist would have allowed

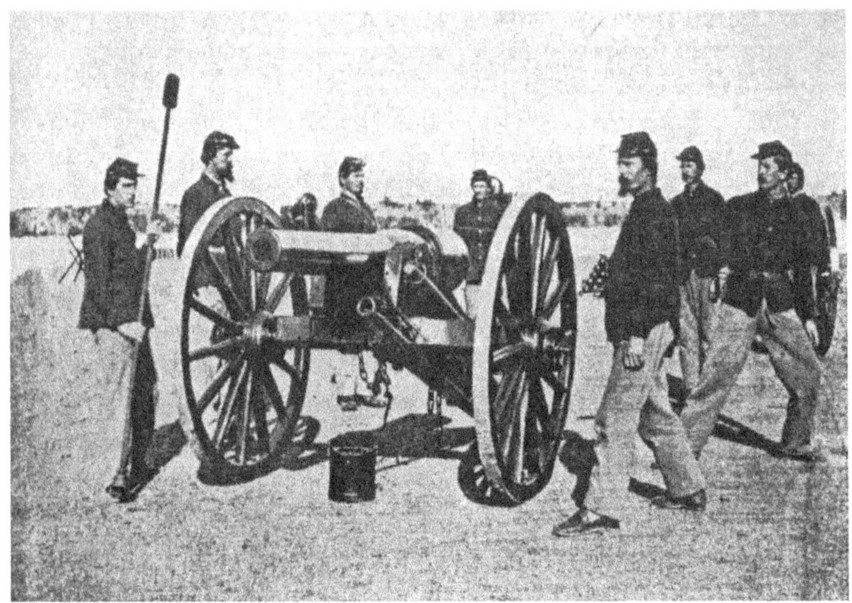

GUN CREW M. B. Brady

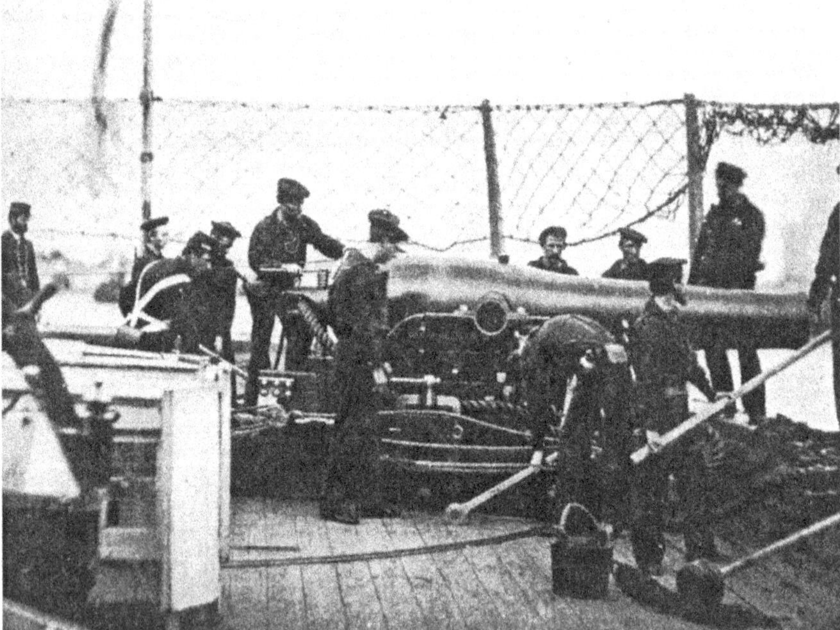

DECK OF U.S.S. MIAMI M. B. Brady

Fig. 1.5 Mathew Brady. Images of the Civil War reprinted in *Hound & Horn* VII, no. 1 (October–December 1933)

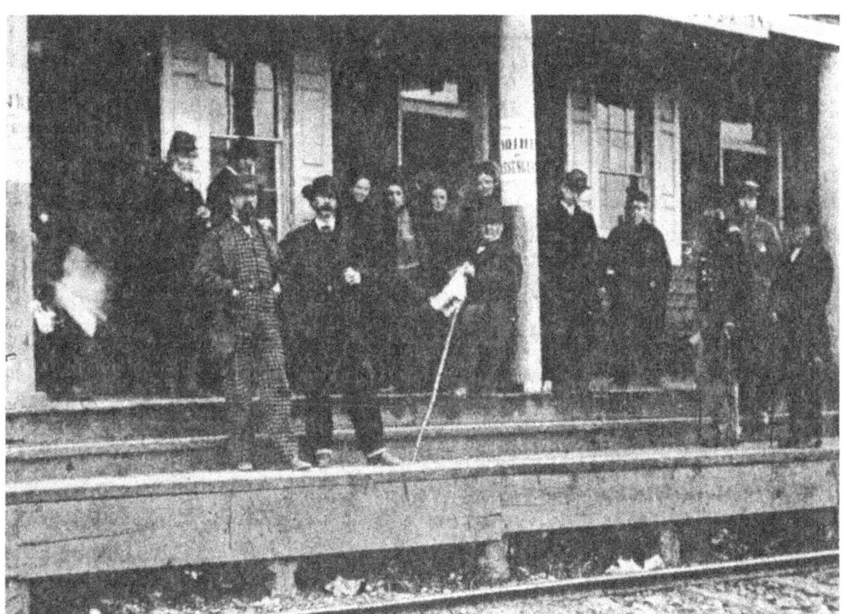

HANOVER JUNCTION, PA. M. B. Brady

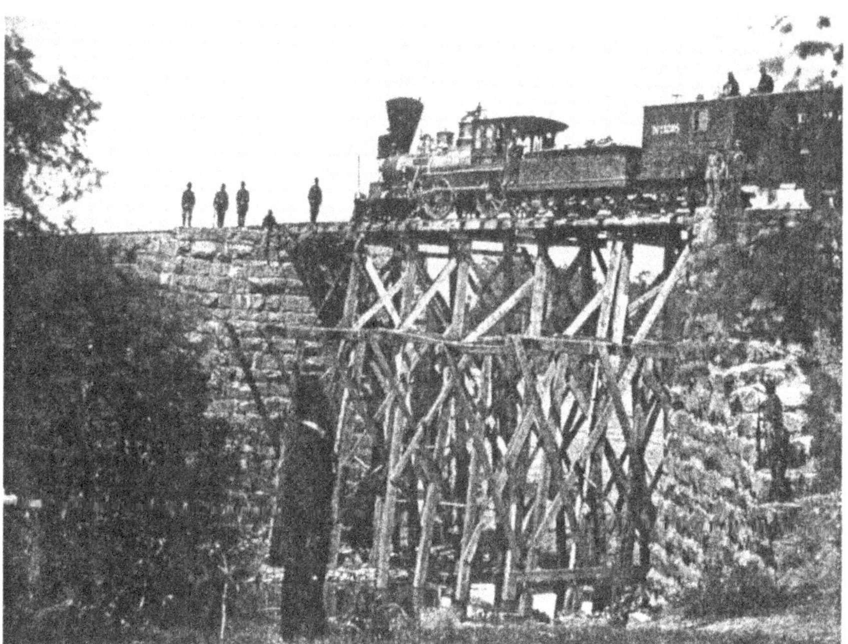

UNITED STATES MILITARY RAILROAD M. B. Brady

Fig. 1.6 Mathew Brady. Images of the Civil War (1865) reprinted in *Hound & Horn* VII, no. 1 (October–December 1933)

> proper. . . . Brady saw his figures less as problems in patterns of light than as subjects, persons whom he allowed to dominate his art because of what he regarded of more importance, the person as a literary value.[81]

Walker Evans was consciously working in the Brady tradition, as Lincoln Kirstein notes in his essay in the book *American Photographs,* which reproduces images from Evans's 1938 show at MOMA. Aspects of his "documentary style" recall Brady's work: Evans's choice of the large-view camera rather than the more common small camera then in use; the stable, frontal point of view; even, flat lighting; the formal quality of the pictures, and the sense that the subject was fully aware of the camera and composing himself before its stare; the consistent positioning of the lens at a respectful distance—all combine to create an appearance of "objectivity," and the sense that a record was being made.

American Photographs presents what Trachtenberg calls a "discourse of images,"[82] demonstrating Evans's awareness of how much sequencing affects significance, how the meaning of images change according to the different ways in which they are combined and juxtaposed. When photographs are arranged and presented in a series, the concept of the image itself is decentralized. The Hungarian artist and designer László Moholy-Nagy celebrated the potential of the photographic series in 1932:

> This is the logical culmination of photography. The series is no longer a "picture," and none of the canons of pictorial esthetics can be applied to it. Here the separate picture loses its identity as such and becomes a detail of assembly, an essential structural element of the whole which is the thing itself. In this concatenation of its separate but inseparable parts a photographic series inspired by a definite purpose can become at once the most potent weapon and the tenderest lyric.[83]

Moholy-Nagy was describing a series made from successive images of the same object, but a similar argument may be applied to a series of images regarding the same subject (the United States, for instance), and thus pertains to *American Photographs,* a series that unifies documentary and art to become both a weapon and a poem.

A DEMOCRATIC MEDIUM

Susan Sontag identified Evans as "the last great photographer to work seriously and assuredly in a mood deriving from Whitman's euphoric humanism."[84] Denis Donoghue asserts that Whitman's moral significance issues from how his poems "restore the dignity of the commonplace,"[85] an effort that would become one of the *de facto* goals of the American documentary movement during the late 1930s. The various groups and individuals who comprised this movement were tacitly united in pursuit of a shared objective: to create a comprehensive record of American life. Doing so, however, involving correcting certain long-standing imbalances, with the result that the record itself reflects glaring biases. Just as Whitman, in his poetry, embraced persons and things previously considered inappropriate subjects for artistic treatment, the documentarians of the thirties tended to focus on the working class and the rural poor, with a special interest in the embattled point of contact between humans and the land. Influenced by its precursor in Russia, the American documentary movement tended to dignify and sometimes even mythologize human labor and leaned toward populism in its implied politics. Later in the decade, documentarians employed by the WPA and other New Deal projects were expected to satisfy a government agenda that sought support for its programs. During those years there was little interest in documenting forms of leisure, for example, which were still considered the province of the elite.

In *Leaves of Grass* Whitman not only celebrates democracy but enacts its processes in the sweeping inclusiveness of his long lines. Sontag again: "[W]ithout the heroic inflection, Evans's project . . . descends from Whitman's: the leveling of discriminations between the beautiful and the ugly, the important and the trivial."[86] The camera itself is a democratic medium; even early on, the apparatus was simple and could be mastered by anyone, and because cameras were inexpensively mass-produced most people could afford one. In his essay entitled "Oppen and Zukofsky, and the Poem as Lens," Hugh Kenner discusses some of the effects that photography has had on the visual arts. As he says, "for the camera as not for the painter, there are no trivial subjects: it receives all equally, accords equal status to all" (166). In other words, light is indiscriminate. As Whitman wrote about the American poet, "He judges not as the judge judges but as the sun falling around a helpless thing."[87] It is important to note, however, that the medium has a peculiar affinity for the commonplace; documented on film, the most ordinary things, simply by being made the object of a camera's gaze, acquire a new value, rendering them uncommon. The camera confers importance: being chosen as a focal point invests objects with a kind of power, since the photographer's choice implies there is something worth looking at. Selected by Evans to frame within his viewfinder, the few shabby, carefully arranged possessions in sharecropper Floyd Burroughs's home become, in *Let Us Now Praise Famous Men,* iconic and sacred (see figure 1.7). Photographs do record chance events; part of their appeal is how they capture for our leisurely inspection the random convergences of isolated streams of activity, but the photographer chooses where to

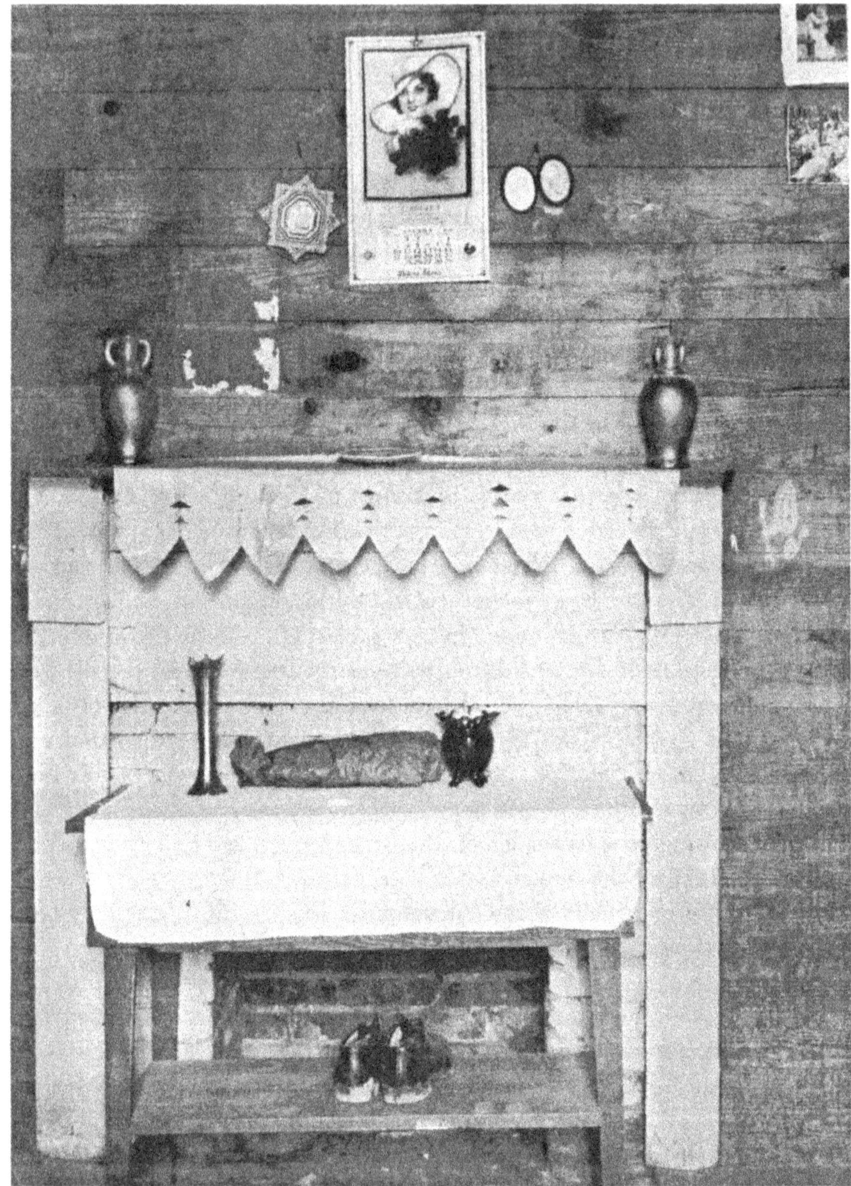

Fig. 1.7 Walker Evans. Fireplace and wall detail in bedroom of [sharecropper] Floyd Burroughs's cabin. Hale County, Alabama (1935 or 1936).
Library of Congress, Prints and Photographs Division, LC-USF342-TO1-008135-A DLC

point the camera and when to press the button, thus composing the image. In Objectivist poetry, as in photography and the majority of artistic media, the artist's choice is integral to the completed work of art.

The damaged lives Charles Reznikoff chose to document in *Testimony*, George Oppen's trust in the "small nouns," Lorine Niedecker's deep study of her acre of rural Wisconsin, Carl Rakosi's representative American types, and Louis Zukofsky's interest in the little words "the" and "and" have their counterparts in the documentarian's concentration on the local, the particular, the commonplace and "typical" American subject, and reflect a similar class bias. Like the documentary photography of the thirties, Objectivist poetry is defined as much by the character of its attentions as by its subject matter. Both the documentary image and the Objectivist image (especially as practiced by Oppen and Reznikoff) enact a similar quality of attention: The observer remains at a respectful distance from his or her subject and feels no compulsion to intrude into the scene or directly comment on its meaning.

SOME CONCLUSIONS

A documentary impulse emerges in children as early as age three. The child experiences it as a form of desire: "I want to know, then tell." According to Robert Coles, what is most important is not the type of expression but the loyalty to the thing itself (that is, sincerity) and to the task of sharing what has been witnessed with others[88]; the documentary impulse is thus ultimately a social and communicative impulse, as well. Photography, especially the "documentary style" of photography epitomized in the United States by Mathew Brady and Walker Evans, was literary in nature; the genre evolved and was refined in tandem with a current of American poetry that began with Emerson's all-seeing eyeball and flowed out through Whitman: a documentary tradition of American poetics that is essentially realistic and humanistic, favoring "the clear physical eye against the erring brain"[89] as a means of access to knowledge of the world. This confluence between emerging currents of poetry and photography in the United States had a profound effect on the American documentary movement of the 1930s. As William Stott so comprehensively demonstrates, the documentary impulse that led to this movement had long been "in the air" of American culture, expressing itself through a multitude of media.

The following chapters focus on the work of three poets practicing some version of Objectivist poetics during those years; Charles Reznikoff, George Oppen, and William Carlos Williams each channeled these documentary currents into his own distinct version of the Objectivist image, and in the process anticipated the important documentary photography of the decade. Moreover, each successfully resisted the sentimentality and nostalgia that would mar such documentary-inspired poetry as Carl Sandburg's *The People, Yes* (1936) and Archibald MacLeish's *Land of the Free* (1938). These three writers shared the conviction that the poet's eye should take a good, hard look out into the world, and that the poet's job is to construct, based on knowledge gained from that experience, a new object that is the poem. Despite significant differences in their literary styles and temperaments, Reznikoff, Oppen, and Williams all express a visual imperative in their work.

Louis Zukofsky's poetry would develop in directions that have more to do with the ear and musical values than with the eye. (Zukofsky believed "the eye is a function of the ear and the ear of the eye."[90]) Nonetheless, evidence of the shaping influence of the documentary genre on Zukofsky's writing in the years between the wars offers a new perspective on early poems such as "To my wash-stand," "'Mantis,' An Interpretation," and the poems in "A" 1–7. Zukofsky has been a poets' poet, revered by other writers if not exactly embraced by readers. Regarding his work in terms of an emerging documentary climate may help clarify the nature of Zukofsky's theoretical and editorial influence on his contemporaries, specifically Oppen and Williams. In this account, Zukofsky figures primarily as a theorist, the filter through which Pound's Imagism reached Oppen and other poets of that generation.

In *Repression and Recovery,* Cary Nelson challenges the conventional view that the 1930s produced only forgettable political poetry. Nelson argues that the poetry of the time "became one of the most dependable sources of knowledge about society and one's place and choices within it."[91] The Objectivist images of Reznikoff, Oppen, and Williams belong to a body of documentary-inflected work that sought to "think with the things as they exist," and to enable readers to do the same. While these three were emphatically not writing "political poetry," their words helped document a highly politicized period in American history. The veracity of Reznikoff's *Testimony,* Oppen's *Discrete Series,* and Williams's *Collected Poems 1921–1931* as sources of social and political knowledge depended upon a documentary sincerity that made it an obligation to speak clearly and accurately about "historic and contemporary particulars." In 1941, in *Let Us Now Praise Famous Men,* James Agee concluded that "more direct, true, and unbiased reporting would be done by a poet."[92] This work had already been begun by these poets, years before.

Chapter Two

Documentary Matters: Charles Reznikoff's 1934 *Testimony*

> Every image of the past that is not recognized by the present as one of its concerns threatens to disappear irretrievably.
>
> —Walter Benjamin

Charles Reznikoff was forty in 1934 when the Objectivist Press published *Testimony*, a slim volume based on transcriptions of law reports. It was a productive year for Reznikoff: In addition to *Testimony*, the Objectivist Press (whose editorial board consisted of Ezra Pound, Louis Zukofsky, and William Carlos Williams) also issued two volumes of his poetry: *In Memoriam: 1933* and *Jerusalem the Golden*, a remarkable output considering that money for literary ventures was hard to come by during the Depression. Unfortunately, the books did not sell well. Many critics—especially those on the Left—responded negatively to *Testimony*, mistaking its apparent objectivity for political neutrality, an unacceptable position during those contentious times. In *Dynamo* ("A Journal of Revolutionary Poetry"), Herman Spector slammed Reznikoff for his reluctance to take sides in the class war. The *Nation* declared that "For sheer brutality there is nothing in literature quite like this little volume." Even Reznikoff's wife, Marie Sirkin, confessed that she did not much care for *Testimony*, preferring instead her husband's more traditional lyric poems.[1]

For someone who seemed to have rather modest personal aspirations, *Testimony* was a tremendously ambitious project, encompassing, as Reznikoff imagined it eventually might, "the life of a people, in mines and on ships, all the activities that the law itself covers, which is pretty nearly everything."[2] In its subsequent form the work would eventually expand to two volumes of verse (each nearly 300 pages) surveying the history of the

United States between 1885 and 1915. The 1934 version of *Testimony* (sometimes referred to as "the prose *Testimony*," an epithet neither useful nor accurate, as I will show), with which I will be concerned almost exclusively here, focuses on the social consequences of an economy based on various forms of slavery. Constructed from court records dating from before the Civil War, it consists of three parts: "Southerners and Slaves," "Sailing-Ships and Steamers," and "East and West." Each presents a numbered sequence of short narratives arranged into titled sections, a sampling of which will give a sense of the subject matter: "Of Murder" and "Of Slaves" (from part one); "Collision," "Hands," and "Passengers" (from part two); and "Gunshot Wounds" and "Machinery" from the last section. It does not make for light reading:

> The negro had been chased for two miles in a summer day by negro dogs. He was found in the bayou, up to his chin in the water, with a scythe blade in his hand. This, at the bidding of the man after him, he threw to the water's edge, and came out. As he did so, the white man struck him upon the head with the heavy butt of a whip, and the dogs jumped upon him and began to bite him. (*Testimony* 1, "Of Slaves," 5)

With notable exceptions, most of the passages in *Testimony* describe acts of violence, and many culminate in such an act. Reznikoff trimmed away the explanatory contexts of these episodes, and his elisions create a charged atmosphere into which violence suddenly erupts, without apparent warning or provocation. The deliberate precision with which the most gruesome details are offered and the matter-of-factness of the presentation make passages such as this one all the more horrible:

> The body was in a clump of post-oak bushes, ten or twelve feet from the road, the left foot over the right one. It was on its back. From the eyes down all the face was gone, the face bones were gone, and the brains had been eaten out of the skull by the hogs. The hogs were eating the body when it was found. There was plenty of blood under the head, in the clothes, and on the ground, but no other wounds on the body, except where the hogs had broken the skin of the fingers. (*Testimony* 1, "Of Murder," 5)

Other narratives describe the events that presumably culminated in a crime, but we are left wondering what actually took place. Sometimes it isn't difficult to imagine:

> She said that her husband was in Boston and had been for four or five years. He asked in what street did he live. She named some place he didn't know anything about. [...] He asked her how long since she left Ireland. She said, "I was in Ireland thirteen weeks ago." At that he heard the child she held under her cloak cry.
>
> "What! have you got a baby?" said he.
>
> "It's none of your damn business," said Bridget, and she walked out into the forward part of the deck trying to quiet the child. Some of the passengers gathered at the door to see what she was out there for, among the horses and cows. She walked to the very bow and stared over the bulwark at the black water. (*Testimony* 2, "Passengers," 3)

Unfortunately, excerpts can't really convey a sense of the collective impact of the pieces that make up *Testimony*. Much of the work's power depends on its serial structure and the accumulating nature of its effects: the way certain themes are reiterated and problematized, and the burden of the details presented in each passage. When one regards *Testimony* as a whole, it becomes clear that the work assumed a hybrid form—a form that integrates prose and poetry, document and art—because it had to; the text addresses a number of needs in American culture at that particular point in time, among them the necessity of creating an American history, and the related desire to establish a shared sense of community in the face of a disintegrating social order. Reznikoff responds to these needs in *Testimony* by creating a text that mediates between the various discourses in which they were materialized: historical records, literature, testimonial narratives, letters, and documentary images.

THE GENESIS OF REZNIKOFF'S "DOCUMENTARY" METHOD

To understand what Reznikoff was up to in *Testimony* it is useful to look at the genesis of the project: In 1928, he began working at *Corpus Juris*, a company producing law books and encyclopedias for lawyers. While sifting though the testimony from hundreds of legal cases, Reznikoff began to imagine how these historical documents might be transformed into literature. He began reading case reports from each state, dating from every year since 1776:

> Once in a while I could see in the facts of a case details of the time and place, and it seemed to me that out of such material the century and a half during which the United States has been a nation could be written

MY COUNTRY 'TIS OF THEE

By

CHARLES REZNIKOFF

ORATORICAL AND POETICAL GESTURES.

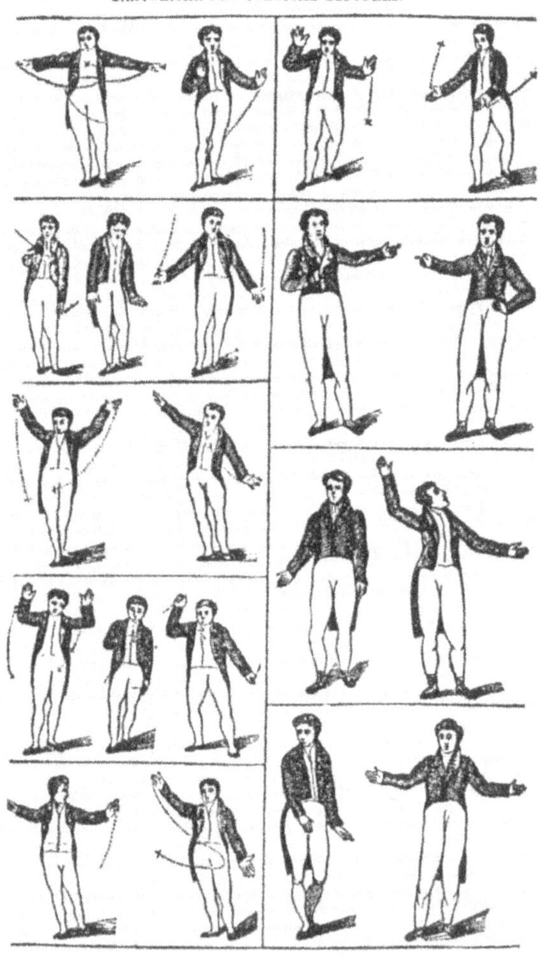

Fig. 2.1 Title page of "My Country 'Tis of Thee" (original title of *Testimony*) as it appeared in the literary quarterly *Contact* (1932)
Courtesy the Estate of Charles Reznikoff.

MY COUNTRY 'TIS OF THEE 107

her home. She walked slowly, but when he said he would whip her or she was afraid she would be ridden against by Mr. Gentry's horse, she walked faster. She said she had run away because she wanted to go to her children.

She would talk to herself and laugh without any one speaking to her as she worked in the fields. She was stubborn and unfriendly, and when she was scolded for it, said she wanted to go to her children; and she ran away time and again. At last her master sold her to Mr. Spencer, and she ran away again.

Spencer caught her and chained her. He asked her why she had run away, and she told him she wanted to go to her children. "I will show those legs," Spencer said, "they shall not run away from me." He had her stripped and staked down on the ground: her feet and hands spread and tied to the stakes, her face downward. Mr. Spencer was calm and took his time; he whipped her from time to time with a plaited buckskin lash about fifteen inches long. He drew some blood, but not a great deal, and then he took salt and a cob and salted her back with it . . .

SIMPLE LAUGHTER.

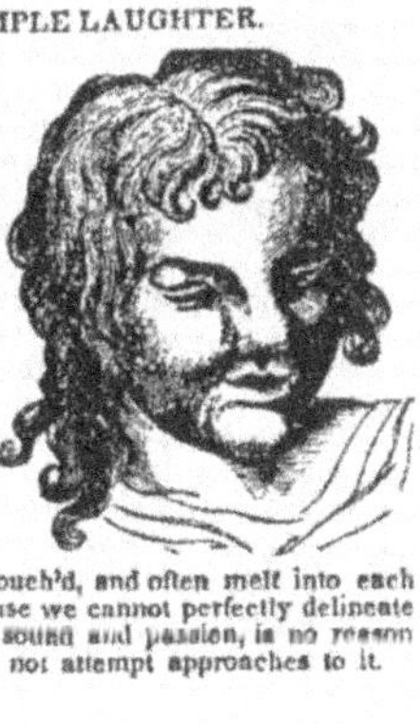

485. RAILLERY—may signify a bantering, a prompting to the use of jesting language; good humored pleasantry, or slight satire; satirical merriment, wit, irony, burlesque. It is very difficult indeed, to mark the precise boundaries of the different passions, as some of them are so slightly touch'd, and often melt into each other; but because we cannot perfectly delineate every shade of sound and passion, is no reason why we should not attempt approaches to it.

Williams was walking in his plantation, when his dogs began a sharp barking in a thicket near by. He went there, and found the camp of what he took to be run-away slaves, but saw none. He got Jackaway, who had a pair of dogs trained to run slaves; the dogs took a trail, and followed on to near Kribs'

Fig. 2.2 From "My Country 'Tis of Thee"
Courtesy the Estate of Charles Reznikoff.

> up, not from the standpoint of an individual, as in diaries, nor merely from the angle of the unusual, as in newspapers, but from every standpoint—as many standpoints as were provided by the witnesses themselves. (Reznikoff, quoted in Kenneth Burke's introduction to the 1934 *Testimony*, xiii)

What Reznikoff describes here looks, at first glance, something like a historical version of a Cubist painting, in which a multiplicity of views challenge our assumptions about visual perception and generate a new understanding of what it means to really see something—in this case, the American past. The innovations of Cubism influenced many writers, some of whom were Reznikoff's contemporaries, such as William Carlos Williams and Gertrude Stein. In the sense that Reznikoff was concerned with presenting multiple viewpoints, this association may be valid. An earlier version of *Testimony*, entitled "My Country 'Tis of Thee" when it appeared in two installments in *Contact* (edited by Williams), does recall Cubist or Surrealist collage in the way it intersperses text with illustrations. Drawn by Charles Sheeler and based on an early American book of rhetoric showing a variety of "oratorical and poetical gestures" (see figures 2.1 and 2.2), these images create an ironic counterpoint when juxtaposed with the gruesome imagery of the court records.

However, as Michael Davidson asserts, what distinguishes the 1934 *Testimony* from Cubist collage is how it "redirects modernism's emphasis on the materiality of aesthetic language to the materiality of social speech."[3] *Testimony* is crafted from materials belonging to the public record, documents generated by the jurisprudential body that mediates between one individual and another in the law courts. Reznikoff's methods of composing this work raise certain questions, which I address in this chapter, concerning the status of documentary materials with respect to "truth" and the nature of mediation itself. Reznikoff's desire to present a multiplicity of viewpoints is, I believe, less of an aesthetic project than a social one and thus in tune with the goals of the American documentary movement, which sought to include all aspects of the nation in its record. In chapter 1 I have tried to give a sense of the breadth of that movement and to describe manifestations of its intriguing symbiosis with modern poetry in the years between the wars. In order to appreciate what Reznikoff accomplished in the 1934 *Testimony* it is necessary to examine the historical context from which this work emerged and the meanings associated with the term documentary during that time.

FRAMING *TESTIMONY*

William Carlos Williams, one of the collective of writers who made up the Objectivist Press, got his friend Kenneth Burke to provide an introduction for *Testimony*. As part of the "frame" contextualizing this work, Burke's introduction, entitled "The Matter of the Document," merits study. Burke begins by describing a phenomenon of the literary landscape circa 1934 when he notes that the traditional distinctions between modes of discourse—such as fiction and nonfiction, prose and poetry, science and art—were in the process of erosion.

> As the "scientific" quality of modern art came more and more into evidence, we began to note a progressive development of fiction towards the "case history." It is only recently that we have become aware of a complementary movement, the movement of the "case history" towards fiction. (xi)

Burke calls attention to the prevalence of a documentary aesthetic in the literature of the thirties when he notes the "progressive development of fiction towards the 'case history,'" a term that reveals its own status as a narrative construction (h*istory*). Given that the distinctions between these forms of discourse were murky and getting murkier, what was a critic (and a reader) to do? How does one judge when the criteria for judgment have shifted so radically? (These are questions that resonate within the text of *Testimony*, as well.) Imagist and especially Objectivist poetics both addressed this problem by focusing on form (objective and therefore measurable) and by creating a new critical vocabulary based upon the new technologies of the time. Judging from the quotation marks deployed liberally throughout Burke's introduction, many formerly definitive terms had come under scrutiny, among them "objective," "subjective," "factual," "actual," "evidence," "truth," "document," "documentary," "poetic," and "testimony." Debate over the status of these terms was surely related to a larger concern: the loss of public confidence in the print medium that occurred in the years following the First World War.[4]

This general mistrust of written language and the growing skepticism about its capacity to tell the truth apparently did not extend to images; in the thirties the photographic image was still widely considered a trustworthy medium. A notorious example will illustrate my point: In 1936 the photographer Arthur Rothstein, on assignment for the Farm Security Administration (FSA) to capture images of the Dust Bowl and document the consequences of years of drought and poor land management, photographed a patch of parched land and a bleached cow skull. When various shots from the same negative were compared, they revealed that Rothstein had moved the skull into various positions in order to get the best shot. We take such manipulations for granted now; even then they were probably routine. In fact, comparisons of images of dead Civil War soldiers taken by Alexander Gardner in 1865 reveal that the photographer rearranged his subjects or mislabeled his photographs to achieve certain effects, even going so far as to misidentify Union soldiers as confederates.[5] Nonetheless, the Rothstein cow skull scandal almost shut down the Photography Unit of the FSA and left the agency scrambling to reassure both the American public and the federal government that documentary photographs could indeed be trusted, that these images were not staged or manipulated or otherwise falsified but were accurate representations of reality.[6] The outcry over the Rothstein incident testifies to the existence of an assumption of trust between the documentary photographer and the viewing public, and shows how unwilling people were to imagine that trust betrayed.

REZNIKOFF AND DOCUMENTARY PHOTOGRAPHY

At this point let me risk an oversimplification: The year *Testimony* was published, the index of "truth" in the United States was the documentary photograph. Photographs have always enjoyed a special status with regard to reality, and literature in the 1930s aspired to that status by seeking to embody photographic forms and to mimic photographic aesthetics. Toward a similar end, Reznikoff purposefully aligned himself with the documentarians of his time and adapted their methods as a means of approaching what Kenneth Burke refers to as "the problem of the 'whole truth.'" In *Testimony*, the text's surface appearance of objectivity, the editorial nature of Reznikoff's relationship to his materials and the collaborative character of the text's composition, as well as his use of serial forms and catalogs as structuring devices, are all aspects of this effort, which I will consider in turn.

Commentators have consistently resorted to photographic analogies to describe the character of Reznikoff's writing. What this illustrates, in part, is the extent to which this new technology had already transformed the vocabulary of modern criticism. Further, it's not difficult to conclude that the favored aesthetic of the era (masquerading, at times, as an objective standard of authenticity) was a photographic one. For instance, in an early (negative) review, Malcolm Cowley calls Reznikoff "astigmatic. He is unable to focus, and lines of splendid verse are lost to sight among low heaps of rubbish."[7] More recently, Paul Auster favorably described the experience of reading a Reznikoff poem as "roughly equivalent to what one feels looking at a photograph."[8] Kathryn

Shevelow explores how Reznikoff translated "prose documentation into a sequence of photographically vivid images" in her study of *Testimony* and *Holocaust.*[9] Even in Reznikoff's early poems one finds the isolated images and deceptively simple diction that prompts such comparisons:

> The shoemaker sat in the cellar's dusk beside his
> bench and sewing machine, his large blackened hands,
> finger-tips flattened and broad, busy.
> Through the grating in the sidewalk over his window,
> papers and dust were falling year by year.
> (from *A Fourth Group of Verse*, 1921)

In a 1939 article about documentary photography, the influential critic Elizabeth McCausland wrote: "a Farm Security Administration photograph of an old woman's knotted and gnarled hands is a human and social document of great moment and moving quality.... The fact is a thousand times more important than the photographer."[10] In verses such as those cited above the poet's role has much in common with that of the documentary photographer: Each directs the lens of his attention away from himself; each is concerned with making a record of something that already exists. Further, both artists strive to efface themselves from what they create: The photographer remains out of sight behind the camera and avoids those effects and angles of vision that call attention to its intrusion; the poet absents himself by avoiding any commentary that might directly convey his own attitudes toward his subject matter. Reznikoff was fond of quoting a rule from eleventh-century Chinese poetry that he believed neatly summed up the Objectivist position: "Poetry presents the thing in order to convey the feeling. It should be precise about the thing and reticent about the feeling."[11] Both photographer and poet thus try to perpetuate an illusion of transparency, creating the impression that reality has been directly transcribed, and the images we see are unmediated by the mechanism of the camera, on the one hand, or by the subjectivity of the poet on the other.

> John Wilson and his younger brother, Cumberland, were cutting timber on a ridge in the woods when Ballentine came up. He had a rifle and a squirrel which he had shot, said that it was hot weather for cutting sticks, and left, going over the ridge. Later, he came out of the woods, and stood watching them.
>
> . . .
>
> (*Testimony* 1, "Of Murder," 2)

A passage like the previous one conveys information in a narrative sequence, certainly, but otherwise does not draw attention to itself as a verbal object, and any sense of a writerly presence is difficult to detect. A comparison of the source documents with the text of *Testimony*[12] reveals much about Reznikoff's working methods and how he achieves an illusion of direct transcription, what Roland Barthes called "writing degree zero." The complaints

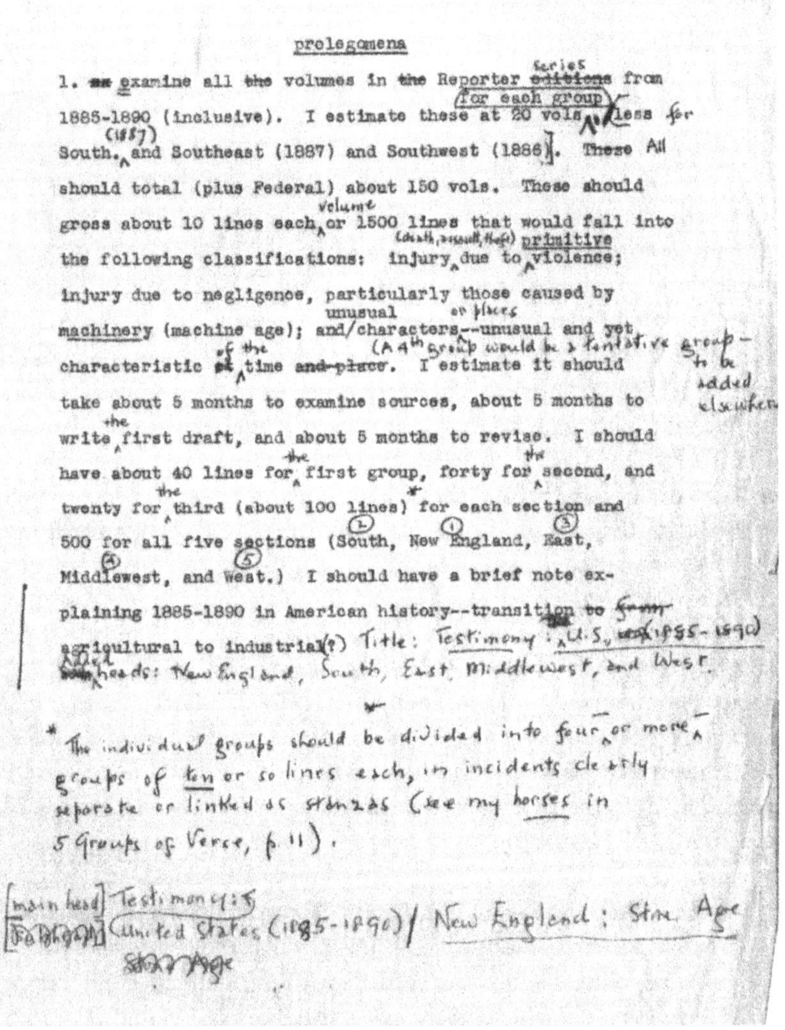

prolegomena

1. examine all volumes in Reporter series from 1885-1890 (inclusive). I estimate these at 20 vols, less for South (1887) and Southeast (1887) and Southwest (1886). All should total (plus Federal) about 150 vols. These should gross about 10 lines each volume, or 1500 lines that would fall into the following classifications: injury (death, assault, theft) due to primitive violence; injury due to negligence, particularly those caused by machinery (machine age); and/characters--unusual and yet unusual or places characteristic of the time. (A 4th group would be a tentative group – to be added elsewhere) I estimate it should take about 5 months to examine sources, about 5 months to write the first draft, and about 5 months to revise. I should have about 40 lines for the first group, forty for the second, and twenty for the third (about 100 lines)* for each section and 500 for all five sections (South, New England, East, Middlewest, and West.) I should have a brief note explaining 1885-1890 in American history--transition to agricultural to industrial(?) Title: Testimony: U.S. (1885-1890) Main heads: New England, South, East, Middlewest, and West.

* The individual groups should be divided into four or more groups of ten or so lines each, in incidents clearly separate or linked as stanzas (see my horses in 5 Groups of Verse, p. 11).

[main head] Testimony: United States (1885-1890) / New England: Stone Age

Fig. 2.3 Charles Reznikoff's "Prolegomena" for *Testimony,* from the poet's working papers. Mandeville Special Collections Library, University of California, San Diego. Courtesy the Estate of Charles Reznikoff.

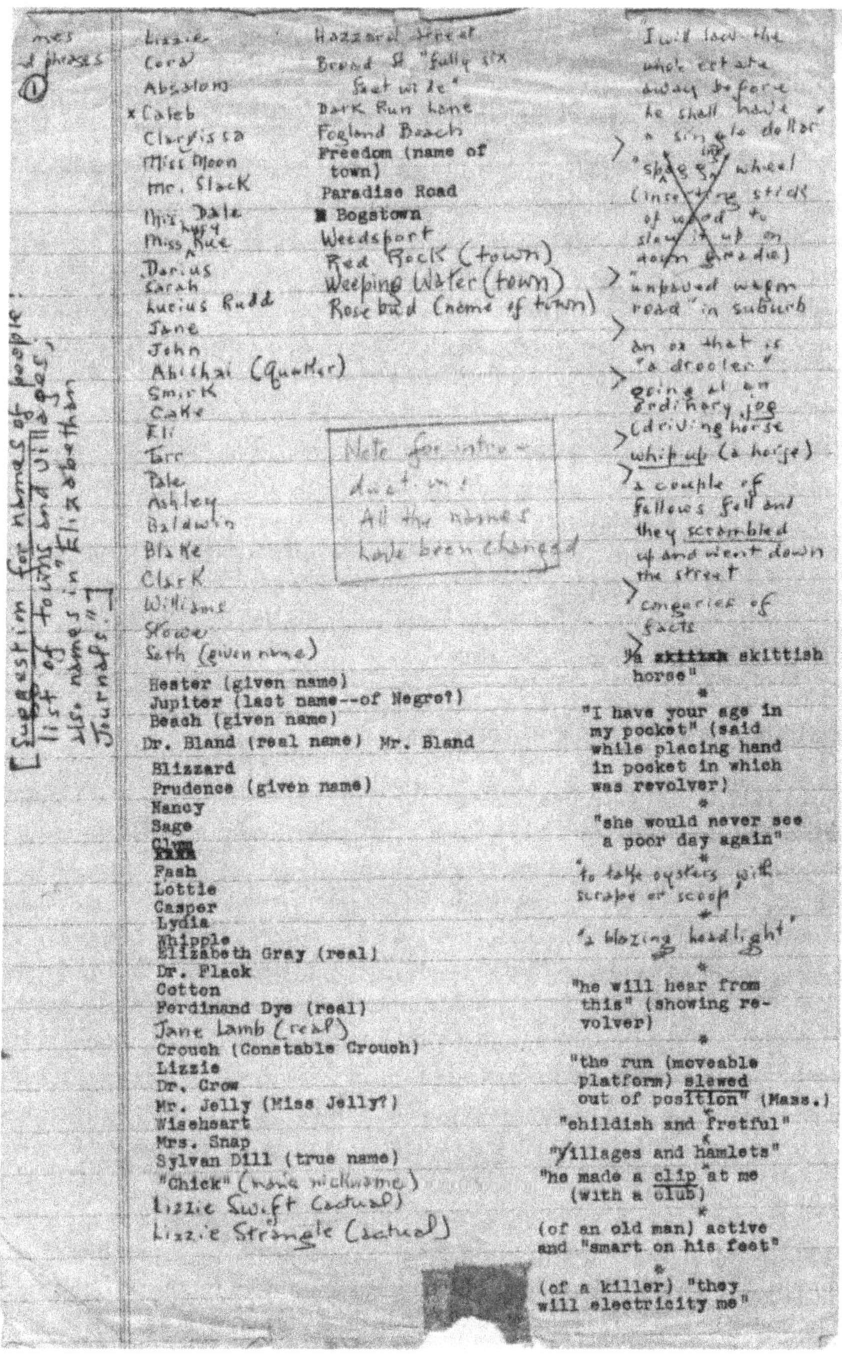
Lizzie
Cora
Absalom
x Caleb
Clarissa
Miss Moon
Mr. Slack
Mrs. Dale
Miss Rue
Darius
Sarah
Lucius Rudd
Jane
John
Abishai (Quaker)
Smirk
Cake
Eli
Tate
Ashley
Baldwin
Blake
Clark
Williams
Stowe
Seth (given name)
Hester (given name)
Jupiter (last name--of Negro?)
Beach (given name)
Dr. Bland (real name) Mr. Bland
Blizzard
Prudence (given name)
Nancy
Sage
Clum
Fash
Lottie
Casper
Lydia
Whipple
Elizabeth Gray (real)
Dr. Flack
Cotton
Ferdinand Dye (real)
Jane Lamb (real)
Crouch (Constable Crouch)
Lizzie
Dr. Crow
Mr. Jelly (Miss Jelly?)
Wiseheart
Mrs. Snap
Sylvan Dill (true name)
"Chick" (man's nickname)
Lizzie Swift (actual)
Lizzie Strangle (actual)

Hazzard Street
Broad St "fully six feet wide"
Dark Run Lane
Fogland Beach
Freedom (name of town)
Paradise Road
Bogstown
Weedsport
Red Rock (town)
Weeping Water (town)
Rosebud (name of town)

Note for intro-duction: All the names have been changed

"I will lose the whole estate away before he shall have a single dollar"
"an ox that is 'a drooler'"
"going at an ordinary jog (driving horse)"
"whip up (a horse)"
"a couple of fellows fell and they scrambled up and went down the street"
"congeries of facts"
"a skittish horse"
*
"I have your age in my pocket" (said while placing hand in pocket in which was revolver)
*
"she would never see a poor day again"
*
"to take oysters with scrape or scoop"
*
"a blazing headlight"
*
"he will hear from this" (showing revolver)
*
"the run (moveable platform) slewed out of position" (Mass.)
"childish and fretful"
"villages and hamlets"
"he made a clip at me (with a club)"
*
(of an old man) active and "smart on his feet"
*
(of a killer) "they will electricity me"

[Suggestion for names of people: list of towns and villages; use names in Elizabethan journals.]

Fig. 2.4 Charles Reznikoff's list of names and phrases for *Testimony*
Mandeville Special Collections Library, University of California, San Diego. Courtesy the Estate of Charles Reznikoff.

of certain reviewers that the work doesn't qualify as literature (in 1952 the scholar and critic Marius Bewley called *Testimony* "a piece of flavorless reporting"[13]) seem to confirm the success with which Reznikoff hid his own hand as a shaper of these materials.

In a note at the beginning of the 1934 edition, Reznikoff describes his method: "I glanced through several hundred volumes of old cases—not a great many as law reports go—and found almost all that follows." "I glanced and found" is a version of "I looked and saw," which Charles Bernstein calls that "twofold action that [Reznikoff's] poems constantly replay."[14] However, this is too casual a description of the labor that actually produced *Testimony*. Reznikoff's working papers reveal the extensive planning and effort that went into this work (see figures 2.3 and 2.4). They also show that Reznikoff changed all the names in the original documents, replacing them with new names that further his designs. In her memoir Marie Sirkin describes how she "could not help grieving over the hours [her husband] spent poring over lawbooks in distant libraries to which he went in all weathers."[15] Reznikoff's "Note" fosters the illusion that *Testimony* is not an aesthetic object but a recovered document, and it is only by replicating Reznikoff's research that can one grasp the extent to which he transformed his source materials.

OBJECTIFYING THE SUBJECTIVE

The construction of an appearance of authorial anonymity would seem to be at odds, however, with Reznikoff's choice of firsthand testimony as the source material for *Testimony*. The documents Reznikoff selected have value precisely because they articulate the perspective of a particular individual at a particular moment in history. In the documentary poem "New Nation" (in *Separate Way*, 1936) Reznikoff composed passages identifying the speakers—"this I, Arthur Barlowe, saw"—to merge with his documentary source texts, as if to stress the importance of the subjective sources of the information. The veracity of these documents issues directly from their status as eyewitness accounts; such testimony is accepted evidence in a court of law. Further, the role of the witness has a crucial significance within Jewish tradition, and many commentators have noted the importance of this tradition to Reznikoff's work.[16] The notion that an "objective" documentary source derives its truth value from subjective experience is a paradox that also characterizes the documentary expression of the thirties; a fact is verified by individual experience but it must transcend the individual's perspective to become "truth"—something meaningful to others.

Kenneth Burke did not, of course, see *Testimony* as a straightforward transcription of legal reports. Throughout "The Matter of the Document" he demonstrates his appreciation of how carefully crafted the text's apparent "objectivity" is, calling *Testimony* sometimes even a "bit too artful in its understatement" (xv). One of the key points that Burke makes in this essay concerns Reznikoff's claim that *Testimony* presents a variety of perspectives, which Burke disputes.

> I have suggested that the material is largely presented from but *one* standpoint, the standpoint of the law court, the "objectivity" of the "evidence," objective in the sense that the writer has given himself to the authority of the material which the court has furnished him, but "subjective," or "selective," or "interpretive," or "biased" in that the law court provides its own principle of selectivity. Whatever individual standpoints they may represent...these bearers of testimony represent in the large the "law court point of view." (xv)

However, the one standpoint is not that of the law court but of Charles Reznikoff, since he selected, arranged, and edited the materials for inclusion in his text, which is entirely shaped by his subjectivity. The different perspectives *Testimony* does present are not those recorded in the documents Reznikoff rescued from the case files but instead are embodied in the different discourses Reznikoff mediates between in this work.

Burke's introduction does suggest the extent to which documentary realism already had become an aesthetic style when Burke refers to Reznikoff's "bare presentation of the records" as well as the "neatness and succinctness and swiftness of effect" in *Testimony.* Praising Reznikoff's "sensitiveness of appraisal, his deftness and accuracy," Burke associates Reznikoff's style with that of the Napoleonic code, the document that reformed the French legal system in accordance with the principals of the French Revolution.

> In a direct style that frequently helps us to realize what Stendhal had in mind when expressing his enthusiasm for the Code Napoleon as a way of statement, [Reznikoff] can contrive by a few hundred "factual" words to stir our feelings and our memories. (xiv)

The Code Napoléon epitomized the linguistic exactitude to which writers such as Stendhal and Flaubert aspired. The more direct and unadorned the style, the more effectively the readers' emotions might be aroused, a technique Reznikoff refined into an art form. "Clarity and precision," the hallmarks of their prose, became part of the criteria for the Imagist poem, thanks to Ezra Pound. Not coincidentally, these qualities are also among those we associate with documentary photographs. Imagism, with its focus on the moment seized and presented in hard-edged language purged of all vagueness and ornamentation, owes much to the photographic aesthetic of the time.

THE INFLUENCE OF POUND'S IMAGISM

Reznikoff came of literary age at the height of Imagism and was profoundly influenced by Pound's formulations. Throughout his life (Reznikoff died in 1976, the year of the nation's bicentennial) he hewed to the Imagist criteria for a poetic language that was clear, concise, free from embellishment, and based on actual speech rhythms. Where he diverged from Pound may be gathered from remarks Reznikoff made in an interview taped in 1973:

> I was just rereading one of Pound's things which they always quote as an example of this kind of writing—call it Objectivist, Imagist—the one about this chap going up in the subway. There are two lines to it, and I see a phrase that is completely unnecessary. Here's the way it reads:
>
> *In a Station of the Metro*
>
> The apparition of these faces in the crowd;
> Petals on a wet, black bough.
>
> Now if I'd been writing this, I'd strike out "the apparition" and write in this way:
>
> Faces in the crowd;
> Petals on a wet, black bough.
>
> and it would've said everything he said.[17]

This passage demonstrates Reznikoff's editorial approach to a text, his practice of selecting the most essential details (faces, petals) and his elimination of everything else in order to concentrate the effects of the language in a manner reminiscent of a Japanese haiku. By excising Pound's metaphor in the phrase "The apparition of these" Reznikoff creates an additional resonance within the poem, allowing the small words to appear without even the announcement of a title, objectifying the apparition of black letters on white paper, like a negative of the poem's image of white petals on a black background. Reznikoff trusts the reader to make connections that are only implicit in the text. Further, he displays his own confidence in showing how even Pound's poetry, which he had admired and learned from, might be improved upon. Reznikoff's treatment of Pound's lines exemplifies his approach to the law reports that eventually became the different versions of *Testimony*.

THE WRITER AS EDITOR

The counterpart of the camera's ability to focus closely on its subject is the elimination of everything beyond the frame; similarly, the activities of selective focusing and elimination were central to Reznikoff's methods in the various manifestations of *Testimony*, works he created principally by editing, isolating key passages and details from a mass of legal testimony, rearranging blocks of text, and excising redundancies. Editing, nearly always an aspect of the writing process, suddenly becomes its principal focus when the writer appropriates and alters preexisting texts in the shaping of a new textual object, making elimination a medium of creation. The insistence upon clarity and precision in much of the literature of that period also highlights the editorial function. In later manuscripts of *Testimony*, Reznikoff referred to himself as the work's editor.[18]

As Burke's introduction to *Testimony* suggests, the thirties witnessed a proliferation of hybrid forms, works that were difficult to classify according to the traditional categories, among them Pound's *Cantos*, Dos Passos's U.S.A. Trilogy (1936), Zora Neale Hurston's *Mules and Men* (1935), and later, Evans and Agee's *Let Us Now Praise Famous Men* (1941). *Testimony* certainly belongs among these. The editorial function of the writer is foregrounded in the creation of hybrid texts, which are edited together from an array of materials. At a time when the dividing lines between genres were increasingly hard to locate, the role of the writer/poet was also being revised.

Much of the photographer's work is editorial as well, beginning with the composition of the picture (one point of focus is chosen, others eliminated), continuing into the darkroom or onscreen where an image may be recropped, and extending into a selection of images from the developed sequence of shots. Reznikoff's presence in *Testimony*, like that of the photographer, resides largely in the nature of his selections and arrangements and the particular biases they inevitably reflect. The evidence of this writer's craft, his fingerprints, may be discovered in the seams of *Testimony*, so to speak, where different materials are brought together and arranged and in how one form of discourse mediates with another. Traces of Reznikoff's poetic sensibilities can be found nearly everywhere in this text, quietly at work in the rhythms of the language and the subtle play of sounds. In the following image, note how the prose narrative drifts almost imperceptibly into poetry:

> The Arab was bound for Desolation Island to take sea-elephant or walrus oil. The sea-elephants were killed by spears here and there on the island. The blubber was taken from the animals wherever killed and carried by the men on their backs over blocks of ice to their hut on the shore to be tried into oil. The land was one of fog and clouds, snow and ice; they saw the sun seldom, and upon the sea on all sides the floating ice. (*Testimony* 2, "Hands," 4)

COLLABORATIVE COMPOSITIONS

The February 1931 issue of *Poetry* magazine included an essay by Louis Zukofsky entitled "Sincerity and Objectification: with Special Reference to the Work of Charles Reznikoff." In the essay's final section, Zukofsky discusses Reznikoff's use of documentary materials as source texts, a practice that situates Reznikoff in the company of other modernist poets such as Marianne Moore, Pound, and Williams, all of whom incorporated quotations and portions of

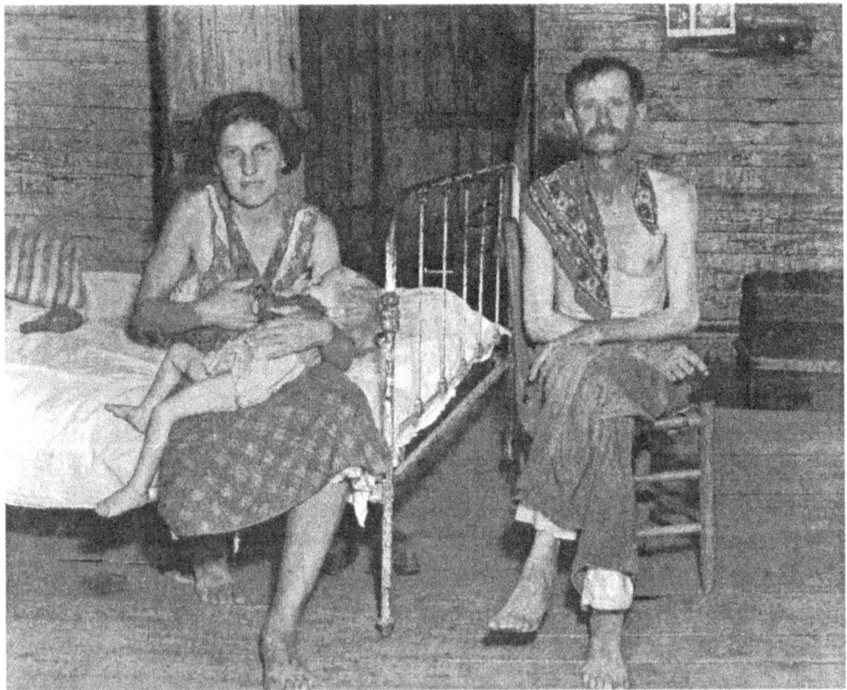

Fig. 2.5 Walker Evans. Bud Fields and his daughter-in-law and granddaughter. Hale County, Alabama (1935 or 1936)
Library of Congress, Prints and Photographs Division LC-USF342-T01-008146-A

documents into their verse. Zukofsky seems at pains to justify a particular poetic stance toward documentary materials because such a stance constitutes, in part, the poet's position with regard to history itself. Zukofsky argues that constructing literature from "found" documents has a social value not only because it saves certain texts from obscurity but because it is preferable to bringing another inferior lyric ("all sorts of personal vagueness") into the world. His insistence that "It is more important for the communal good that individual authors should spend their time recording and objectifying good writing wherever it is found"[19] reflects the time's emphasis on social solutions as well as Zukofsky's own Marxist tendencies during the thirties. The stance toward documentary materials that he valorizes issues from the Objectivist conception of the poet as craftsperson, who constructs a verbal object (the poem) out of the available materials of language: "Interested in craft, Reznikoff has not found it derogatory to his production to infuse his care for significant details and precision into the excellent verbalisms of others."[20]

That's one way of describing what an editor does. Choosing to craft literature out of the "excellent verbalisms of others" is to embark upon an editorial project, an essentially collaborative process. A work such as *Testimony* qualifies as a collaborative composition in the same sense that a documentary photograph might. Walker Evans's famous photographs in *Let Us Now Praise Famous Men* (a collaboration of text and images) were taken with the full consent of Evans's subjects. While Bud Fields ("Bud Woods" in the book) and his daughter-in-law Ivy may not have known or agreed with all the uses to which their images would eventually be put, these Alabama sharecroppers were fully aware of Evans's camera and made preparations to compose themselves before it, demonstrating their complicity or collaboration in the picture-making process (see figure 2.5). Similarly, the witnesses whose testimony Reznikoff made use of knew that the words they chose to utter in court would become part of the public record. Reznikoff's method of composition in *Testimony* had a distinct advantage: The materials from these casebooks were in the public domain and therefore available to anyone. Accessibility was only part of their appeal, however. The "historic particulars" (Zukofsky's phrase) contained in these documents afforded Reznikoff a means of presenting a history of the United States without resorting to traditional narrative structures.

SERIAL FORM

The importance of the series in Reznikoff's work affords another opportunity to explore its affinities to photography. Reznikoff's poems are more frequently identified by numbers than by titles, emphasizing how each functions as a component of a series, a part of a larger whole. Further, with subsequent editions of his books, Reznikoff habitually rearranged the order of the poems, suggesting endless possibilities for recombination. The preliminary installments of *Testimony* (entitled "My Country 'Tis of Thee") that appeared in *Contact* and in Zukofsky's *An "Objectivists" Anthology* (1932) consisted of two groups of numbered passages, which Reznikoff later recombined to create the first chapter of *Testimony*. In constructing the 1934 *Testimony* Reznikoff rearranged sections, subtracting some parts and adding others, emphasizing the serial nature of the work's arrangement and the potential for recombination of its component parts.

Charles Bernstein reminds us that "Reading Reznikoff formally means attending to the relation of the part to the whole (and the whole to the part) in his work, along lines that also suggest the relation of the shot to the sequence (in film and photography)."[21] Evans and other documentary photographers such as Dorothea Lange conceptualized their work in terms of sequences rather than as single shots; the isolation of an image has the effect of aestheticizing it, removing it from context and making it an art object, a practice at odds with the goals of documentary itself. (See also chapter 3 on Evans's serial composition and Oppen's use of the discrete series.)

POETIC CATALOGS

While Burke largely approved of the starkness of *Testimony*, the "bare presentation of the records," he criticized Reznikoff for

> giving himself over to embellishment of the "poetic" sort, as in his catalogue, "River and Seas, Harbors and Ports." These efforts seem less effective in themselves, though they may serve to restore us for the pointedness of his more incisive manner. (xiv)

The passage Burke refers to, which concludes the second chapter entitled "Sailing-Ships and Steamers," is the longest in that section and differs strikingly in tone and substance from the rest of the text. An example:

> Standing at the helm as the ship goes up the river in the evening, between daylight and candlelight, gawking at the town; a cask of wine brought alongside, slung in a lighter to be hoisted on board, the mate himself at the tackle-fall, and then at the point of passage over the waist of the ship, which is high, the cask suddenly turning athwartships, slipping out of the

> slings, stoven, and the wine lost; messes of salted halibut and rice or beans, a helping of duff, coffee or tea morning and evening and a weekly allowance of spirits; jogging at the pump, pulling the ropes, going aloft; (*Testimony* 2, "Rivers and Seas, Harbors and Ports")

The detail of the broken wine cask is the only destructive particular in the entire section, in marked contrast to the mayhem and murder that surround this section of the book. "Rivers and Seas, Harbors and Ports" contains a series of catalogs, which list the names of ships and those aboard them, and the rich and strange array of goods stored in their holds ("six seroons of indigo; pigs of lead, moys of salt, and frails of raisins"). The longest catalog by far features the weather and water conditions (the movements of clouds, the changing moon, the behavior of the air and water) that sailors contend with as part of their work. It reads, in part:

> the wind east and light, the night dark and without moon; the night dark and cloudy with a fresh wind from the southwest, showers and some mist, the sea heavy and confused, running from the northwest and from the southwest; the night dark and then a drizzling rain, the sea heavy and the ship pitching a good deal, misty, a pretty thick night, small thick rain; (56)

In these lines narrative as a shaping device has been temporarily jettisoned in favor of an extended enumeration of particulars. As we read, sentences give way to short notational phrases until, by the end, Reznikoff has abandoned everything except a handful of nouns that trace the ships' return from the open sea: "bays, inlets, rivers, harbors and ports" (56).

The catalog is a key principle of documentary organization; it is inclusive and open-ended, its serial arrangement is inherently democratic, and its effects depend upon an accumulation of details rather than an imposed structure or hierarchy of information. Cecelia Tichi's observation about Dos Passos's use of this device seems also to apply here; in his U.S.A. Trilogy the list "originates from the premise that the world is a complex structure of component parts, each existing in a precise, discrete relation to the others."[22] The text of Pare Lorentz's hugely popular documentary film *The River* (1936), which James Joyce praised as "the most beautiful [prose] I have heard in ten years,"[23] uses this device in its lyrical invocation of the names of American waterways, "every rivulet and brook, creek and rill" and the places they run through, in flowing language that conveys the gathering force of the water through an accumulation of named particulars.

The text of *The River* gets some of its lyrical mileage by echoing deeply familiar Biblical catalogs, and I think it is worth noting that the Old Testament was an essential source text for Reznikoff throughout his life. The Bible is, as Robert Coles reminds us, also a documentary text.[24] One cannot encounter a catalog in twentieth-century American literature without thinking, too, of Walt Whitman, who adapted the Biblical convention of enumeration to his own singular, secular needs. As I note in chapter 1, Whitman served as a medium by which a documentary impulse entered American poetry. Reznikoff denied that Whitman was one of his poetic influences ("I don't particularly care for him"[25]), and it's not hard to imagine what Reznikoff would have disapproved of—Whitman's self-promotion and his capacious subjectivity; his "barbaric yawp" seems the polar opposite of what Reznikoff called his own "still, small voice."[26] Nevertheless, in their own ways, Whitman and Reznikoff were each mining a documentary vein. Vision is a privileged sense for each of these poets, and there is a solicitousness to their attentions, a quality the poet Charles Tomlinson puts his finger on when he notes how each "succeeds in noticing things that seem not to matter and in isolating them with art."[27]

To return to Burke's criticism of this passage: I agree with him that "Rivers and Seas, Harbors and Ports" provides a respite from the relentless brutality of the rest of *Testimony*. However, calling the poetic effects in this passage an "embellishment" seems off the mark. What Reznikoff has accomplished is the very opposite of embellishment, in fact. Reznikoff has taken the narrative materials of these testimonies and successively trimmed away all the supporting structures upon which narrative traditionally relies. The lists we are left with, of goods, ships, and weather conditions, document history in an alternative way, challenging the notion that narrative alone has historical validity. Narrative generates a plot structure to which historic particulars may be subsequently forced to conform; in seeking to explain events, narrative may actually distort and falsify them in the service of its own interior logic. In a courtroom, defendants are spared or hung on the basis of whose lawyer tells a better story. Reznikoff's lists prove that the presentation of one object after another after another can generate form and meaning in a manner both poetic and historically valid.

USEFUL TRUTHS

Accumulation doesn't equal objectivity, of course, just as testimony—even volumes of it—necessarily presents only a partial truth. Despite Reznikoff's belief that something objective ("the material of life") might be constructed from a plurality of perspectives, Burke concludes by locating the "truth" of

Testimony (that is, "its usefulness to living") not in the documentary materials Reznikoff assembles but rather in "the vein of sympathy that underlies [Reznikoff's] work" (xvi). This sympathy is certainly palpable in the poetry; note how the following image is suffused with tenderness despite the apparent "objectivity" and reticence of its presentation:

> In the shop, she, her mother, and grandmother,
> thinking at times of women at windows in still streets,
> or women reading, a glow on resting hands.
> (1919, from *By the Well of Living and Seeing*)

As in the pieces comprising *Testimony*, emotion emanates not from the visual image per se but from the way Reznikoff deftly orchestrates the rhythms and tonal qualities of the words that present that image. Discussing his working methods, Reznikoff reveals the extent to which emotion governed his choices: "I went at it very simply, without any of this deep penetration. I read a case and it moved me, I mean the facts which are very seldom portrayed.... I wasn't trying to do anything philosophical, I just went by what moved me."[28]

The success with which documentary photography during the 1930s aroused the sympathies of more financially secure viewers on behalf of the impoverished and dispossessed had the very tangible result of creating what Benedict Anderson has termed an "imagined community," a sense of nationhood where none had previously existed. William Stott reminds us that

> hunger and Dust Bowl were not common experience. The people reading of them, or seeing photos or films of them, were not hungry, not Okies, not sharing the experience. And yet they cared. The thing that held American society together in the thirties was not documentary, though documentary gave it occasion to take hold. It was imagination with a strong fellow feeling; it was human sympathy.[29]

The film producer John Grierson believed that the documentaries of the thirties helped unify the British people in preparation for fighting World War Two. The sense of nationhood generated by this genre and how it was concretized in action was undeniably instrumental in helping the United States survive the upheavals of that difficult decade that preceded the war.[30] Prior to the thirties, social reform movements had discovered the effectiveness of documentary images in generating sympathy for the poor among the more comfortable classes who suddenly witnessed, to echo the title of photographer and social reformer Jacob Riis's famous 1890 book, "how the other half lived." Reznikoff's own experiences as a Jew and as the child of immigrants made him keenly empathetic toward victimized groups, a quality evident in all of his writing; these sympathies are powerfully conveyed, as Burke recognized, by the images in *Testimony.*

LEWIS HINE'S "HUMAN DOCUMENTS"

> Jacob Robinson was the cabin-boy on a schooner. He had no mittens, neither woolen nor cotton, nor thick socks; he had a woolen shirt, but no heavy frock. Off the coast, nearing New York on the way from Curaçoa [sic], the weather became stormy. The cook was placed at one of the pumps and Jacob at the other. The waves burst over the deck and he was often knee-deep in the freezing water.
>
> At dawn the schooner was in the bay. Jacob's feet were numb and he could hardly hobble about. As the ship went up the river to her wharf, the sky became clear and blue; and, except where the shadows of houses and smoking chimneys were on the snow, the white roofs and streets of the city glistened.
>
> Jacob was left alone on the ship. Suddenly the church bells began to ring, for it was Christmas day. His sister's house, from which he had run away, was only a few blocks off. He hobbled and crawled—with bare hands in the snow—through the streets along which cheerful people, stiff in their best, were beginning to walk. (*Testimony* 2, "Water and Ice," 1)

Many passages in *Testimony* invite comparisons with the work of the photographer Lewis Hine. Hine's work for the National Child Labor Committee, completed between 1904-1918, was rediscovered during the 1930s, and Elizabeth McCausland declared Hine the link between the documentary work of Mathew Brady and the new practitioners of the "documentary style," such as Berenice Abbott and Walker Evans. Born in the Midwest in 1874, Hine attended the University of Chicago, where he became interested in social reform. Eventually he took a teaching position at the Ethical Culture School in New York City.[31] Hine's teaching was influenced by the pedagogical theories of John Dewey, a professor at the University of Chicago with whom Hine may well have studied.

Dewey's theories of aesthetic reception distinguish between what he termed "recognition" and "perception": the latter is what the artist strives to effect through his or her art, a condition in which the viewer actually undergoes the experience of the artist. Alan Trachtenberg has written that Hine

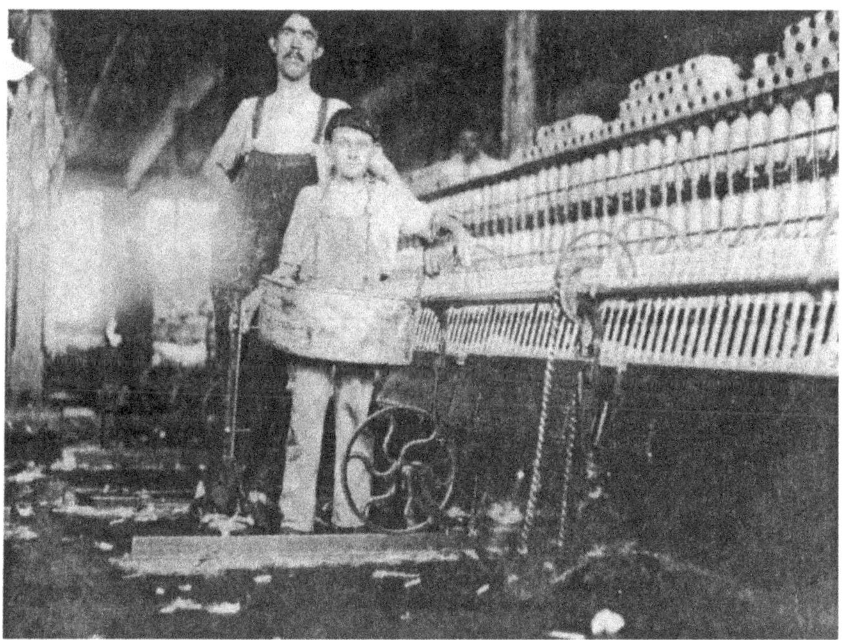

Fig. 2.6 Lewis Hine (1910). Hine's original caption accompanying photograph reads: "Street Bretzau, who is a 'Tube-boy' in the mule-room of Richmond Spinning Mill, East Lake. Mule spinning is apparently more dangerous than ring spinning. (See bandaged finger.) Photo during working hours. Location: Chattanooga, Tennessee." Library of Congress, Prints and Photographs Division LC-USZ62-25111

> enlarged the reformist idea of the social survey to embrace the process of communication itself, inventing presentational forms through which social information might become the viewer's own concrete experience—not facts "out there," in a distant realm, or facts to incite pity, but visual facts as the occasion for awakening the viewer's awareness of and imaginative empathy with the pictured others, and thus the viewer's own social being.[32]

In clarifying what Dewey's concept of perception meant for Hine's work, Trachtenberg describes, in effect, aspects of Reznikoff's project in *Testimony*. By creating an illusion of direct presentation, unmediated by authorial presence, Reznikoff, too, sought to motivate "the viewer's awareness of and imaginative empathy with the pictured others." The similarities between Hine's and Reznikoff's projects extend to the way Reznikoff chose to structure his materials; from its earliest incarnations, *Testimony* suggests a documentary survey in its presentation of catalogs of abuse.

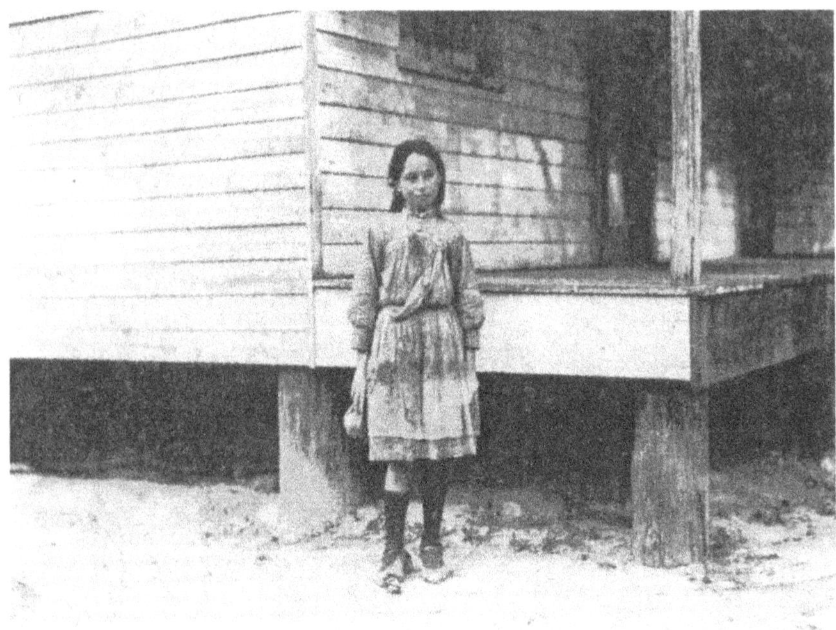

Fig. 2.7 Lewis Hine (1911). Hine's caption reads: "Lillian Dambrinio, an eleven-year-old shrimp picker in Peerless Oyster Co. She is an American and lives here. Says picking makes her hands sore. (Note the condition of her shoes. One worker told me, 'The acid in the shrimp eats the shoes off your feet.') She says she earns a dollar a day when shrimp are big. Goes to school, but not when the factory is busy. Location: Bay St. Louis, Mississippi."
Library of Congress, Prints and Photographs Division LC-DIG-nclc-00903

The ability of Hine's images to affect social change relied upon their capacity to elicit sympathy in the viewer as well as to implicate the viewer in the specific reality that they disclose. Reviewing his volume *Poems* (1920), one critic scolded Reznikoff for "giving us verbal photographs of objects that make us shut our eyes and clamp our noses."[33] Hine faced the challenge of having to convince people of a truth they preferred not to acknowledge: that this child was injured while spinning the thread that holds your shirt together. To do so, Hine taught himself to use a camera, believing this was the most effective way to accomplish his goals: "If I could tell the story in words, I wouldn't need to lug a camera."[34] But the story could not be told with photographic images alone. Hine's photographs were published with his own captions providing information the bare images could not supply (see figures 2.6, 2.7, and 2.8). The six-volume *Pittsburgh Survey* (1904–1914), which used Hine's photographs to document the labor and living conditions of working class people in

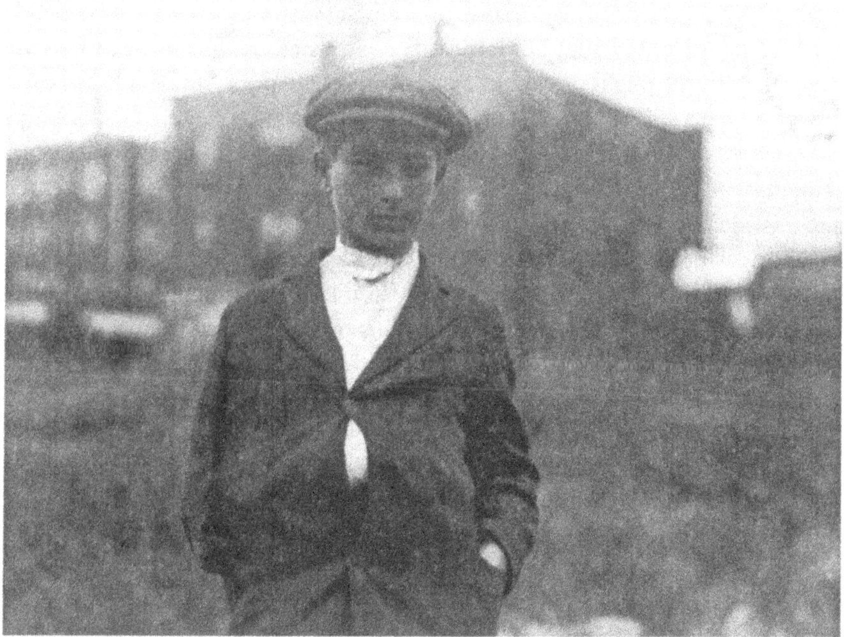

Fig. 2.8 Lewis Hine. Hine's caption reads: "Jo Frank, 38 Blaine St. Broke his arm in mill-belt accident. Said 16 years. Location: Fall River, Massachusetts" (1916) Library of Congress, Prints and Photographs Division, LC-DIG-nclc-03010

that city, relied on both words and images "to make the town real—to itself."[35] In Hine's images, which he often referred to as "human documents," the damaged bodies of his subjects and the identifying details in his captions testify to the victimization of these individuals ("I have always been more interested in persons than in people," Hine once said) and to the larger social injustices perpetrated against the poor and working classes. Reznikoff, the son of Jewish immigrants who had been industrial workers, discloses many similar abuses in the pages of *Testimony.* Reznikoff extends Hine's project, in a sense, by enabling the people under similar conditions to speak for themselves by bringing their testimony to light.

DOCUMENTARY ACTIVISM

In *They Must Be Represented*, her study of the politics of documentary, Paula Rabinowitz notes how the genre is more performative than fiction since it seeks to not only represent reality but to change it by arousing feeling, thought, and action.[36] Lewis Hine's photographs were instrumental in influencing public opinion, though federal regulations regarding child labor would not be passed until 1938, under Franklin D. Roosevelt's administration. Reznikoff's persistent concern with the plight of workers and victimized persons can be inferred from his writing; his efforts to create a type of documentary literature, one that forces the reader to confront the violent realities of American life, should not be faulted because it doesn't endorse a specific revolutionary program. Criticism, such as Herman Spector's, that accuses Reznikoff of merely presenting social problems without analyzing their causes or suggesting possible (i.e., Marxian) solutions fails to appreciate how and why Reznikoff purposefully aligns himself, in *Testimony*, with the documentarians of his time. The performative nature of documentary expression depends upon an assumption that people will be moved (a word Reznikoff used, as I have noted, to describe his responses to these testimonies) by what they see and thus motivated to initiate change. Reznikoff trusted the reader to draw the appropriate moral conclusions based on the evidence, which is one reason why he did not include the outcomes of these cases as determined by a judge or jury. As Michael Heller explains in reference to the later poetic editions of *Testimony*,

> The intention of these poems, it must be insisted on, has nothing to do with a suspension of judgment or with the shallow themes of artistic and moral relativism which seem to be in fashion today. On the contrary: Reznikoff's intention is to provide the occasion for accurate understanding and judgment.[37]

By creating, through his writing, opportunities for informed judgment on the part of his readers, Reznikoff demonstrates his trust in people's abilities to judge for themselves and to take action once they achieve understanding, a trust largely absent from much of the proletarian literature of the thirties. To echo Heller's point, there is no question of suspending our own sense of judgment when we confront evidence such as this:

> . . .
> Spencer caught her and chained her. He asked her why she had run away, and she told him she wanted to go to her children. "I will show those legs," Spencer said, "they shall not run away from me." He had her stripped and staked down on the ground: her feet and hands spread and tied to stakes, her face downward. Mr. Spencer was calm and took his time; he whipped her from time to time with a plaited buckskin lash about fifteen inches long. He drew some blood, but not a great deal, and then he took salt and a cob and salted her back with it. (*Testimony* 1, "Of Slaves," 3)

VIOLENT TIMES

Reznikoff was criticized for the unrelenting darkness of *Testimony*. Some commentators were bothered by the apparent bias of the material toward "all that is most sordid and terrible in American life."[38] In that respect, *Testimony* mirrored the times: The social order was disintegrating; one in four individuals was out of a job; masses of people wandered the country in search of work; and violent crime rates spiked sharply.[39] In an issue of *Contact* (1932) where one of the preliminary versions of *Testimony* appeared, Nathanael West contributed "Some Notes on Violence," which have some bearing on this matter. West wonders,

> Is there any meaning in the fact that almost every manuscript we receive has violence for its core?... We did not start with the ideas of printing tales of violence. We now believe that we would be doing violence by suppressing them.... In America violence is idiomatic. Read our newspapers. To make the front page a murderer has to use his imagination; he also has to use a particularly hideous instrument.[40]

That might have been written yesterday. It can be no coincidence that the last section of *Testimony* is titled "Depression"; Reznikoff finished the work in the midst of the Depression, and he locates, by implication, the roots of the current economic crisis in the nation's violent past.

Based upon the evidence of the majority of passages in *Testimony*, it would be easy enough to argue for an ironic reading of the work's epigraph, which Reznikoff retained through various versions of *Testimony*: "Let all bitterness, and wrath, and anger, and clamour, and railing, be put away from you, with all malice" (from Ephesians 4: 31). However, Reznikoff's decision to change his original title, "My Country 'Tis of Thee," to the more neutral *Testimony* implies that irony amounted to a kind of commentary he sought to avoid in his work. Reznikoff may have retained his Biblical epigraph because he meant its admonishments to be taken sincerely, in the manner of a sermon.

IMAGES OF COMMUNITY

The first section of *Testimony*, entitled "Southerners and Slaves," presents images of a slave economy that relies on violence for its perpetuation. The other pieces in this section show how the inherent barbarity of the institution taints not only the relations between master and slave but is transmuted into the similarly violent and exploitative relationship between boss and laborer, resulting in a general debasement and endangerment of all human life. We also see images of white southerners murdering one another, episodes of black-on-black violence, and children of both races damaged and suffering.

Despite its nearly relentless brutality, *Testimony* also presents several images of community—examples of what people can accomplish when they work together—all the more powerful for being based upon actual incidents. The final and longest piece in "Southerners and Slaves" concerns not an instance of violence but the collective action of both blacks and whites banding together in defiance of the law:

> In the fall, Francis Troutman, who had been told that his grandfather's run-away slaves were in Marshall, Michigan, went there to find and arrest them. He had Dickson, a deputy sheriff of the county, come with him and his companions, Ford and Lee, to the home of the slaves. As they walked up the path to the door, Adam Crosswhite and his son Johnson, two of the run-aways, ran out. One went to the left and the other to the right, but they were followed, and, overtaken, came back to the house. (*Testimony* 1, "Of Slaves," 6)

Soon a crowd assembles to resist the seizure of Adam Crosswhite and his family, and Reznikoff shows us this is a mixed group, in more than one sense: "One hundred or more men and boys had gathered, fifteen or twenty of whom were blacks or mulattoes." Whether this resistance is spurred on by abolitionist sentiment or simply a sense of territory isn't made entirely clear. Threats are made and various weapons brandished, but no physical injuries occur. What is most remarkable about this passage is how legal discourse is used, in effect, against itself to mediate this quarrel and resolve it nonviolently:

> Combstock, a white man, shouted, "You cannot have the negroes!"
>
> Troutman, looking him full in the face, asked, "Why not?"
>
> Combstock, pointing to the crowd, said, "You can't take them by moral, physical, or legal force, and you might as well know it first as last, and the quicker you leave the ground, the better for you."
>
> Gorham took up Combstock's words and offered the following resolution: "Resolved, that these Kentuckians shall not take the Crosswhite family by virtue of moral, physical, or legal force." This was passed by acclamation and with much cheering.

In one sense this constitutes a parody of due process of law; however, it also illustrates an instance in which the moral authority of the community takes precedence over the law—as one character says, "public sentiment [is] above the law"—and the medium of legal discourse is instrumental in bringing this about. This was how the United States was founded, after all.

Another rare example from *Testimony* of the capacity of the community to literally engineer its own salvation occurs in the second section, "Sailing-Ships and Steamers." The majority of these maritime "vignettes" show the horrendous treatment deckhands suffer aboard ship:

> Captain Pride had once beaten a sailor until he was flat on the deck. When he got to his feet, he began to run forward; he was brought back by the mate, upon Captain Pride's order, and beaten again until he was all bloody. This time he was tied to the rigging by his hands, and as the master beat him he sank down, lifted up only by his hands. ("Hands," 10)

That the captain is referred to here as "the master" emphasizes the virtual slavery these sailors endure. However, the sailors themselves often display the same callousness and cruelty toward one another.

One remarkable exception to this Hobbesian view of life tells the story of a large unnamed ship that loses its rudder in a storm and is foundering helplessly. Through the combined ingenuity of both passengers and crew, a problem of how to reconstruct a replacement steering mechanism is solved, a process described in meticulous detail:

> They brought from the forward part of the ship a chain that weighed about sixty pounds to the link, and let it down into the "steerage deck" through a hole cut above it. Though the cone turned with the shaft and the swell of the sea kept the cone always turning, they managed to wind around it enough of the great chain to make a cylinder or drum. The links on the inner coil sank in between the ribs of the cone, keeping the chain from slipping and easing the strain on the lashings—the links were lashed to each other and to the base of the cone by smaller chains. The ends of the great chain were then carried to two strong posts or bitts which came up through the "steerage deck", a turn taken around each, and the ends joined to tackles. These were fastened to the sides of the ship and manned for taking up the slack and easing away as the wheel might turn the rudder shaft. Smaller chains, fastened between the bitts and the cylinder or

> drum, joined the great chain to the wheel—the size of the shackles such that a break would be in them, not in the great chain or its lashings.
>
> The men worked during Saturday night and Sunday; and late Sunday afternoon, the ship was brought up to the sea and put upon her course. (*Testimony* 2, "Water and Ice," 3)

Among other things, it pays to notice here the phrase "the great chain," which recurs four times in this passage. In sifting through the vast legal record from which he drew his materials for *Testimony*, Reznikoff made choices that were emotionally motivated. This narrative of the salvation of the ship surely appealed to him, in part, because of the image he encountered right there in the record: that potent symbol of community, the democratic ideal of the great chain of society, a metaphor with a long history.

RESISTING SYMBOLISM, OR SOMETIMES A GIRDER IS JUST A GIRDER

However tempting it may be to take the symbolist route, Reznikoff's meticulous description of the labor and ingenuity involved in the construction of this replacement piece keeps the focus of the passage squarely on the engineering problem itself; the many mechanical details work to ground the narrative in reality, so to speak, and prevent it from drifting off into the realm of symbolism. In this manner, *Testimony* keeps reminding us that the nature of our concerns is right before our eyes: These are the sicknesses of our culture; here are the available materials and resources through which we can heal these diseases. Symbols, on the other hand, serve to distract us from our responsibilities to one another by enlisting the facts in the service of an overarching idea that alters their meaning and falsifies their truths. The images of community in *Testimony* are directly presented; they do not re-present a larger, symbolic notion of Community. As was increasingly obvious during the 1930s, symbols can be used to motivate masses of people to do terrible things.

It is worth remembering that in Germany, the year before *Testimony* appeared, the Nazis had ordered the burning of all books by Jewish writers. An awareness of the mortality of the text, the vulnerability of these materials, contradicts the conventional view of literature as an immortal realm and places a special value on rescuing and preserving the written repositories of culture. In such a dangerous political climate, the materials containing cultural histories suffer the same fates as human bodies do: They may be suppressed, silenced, and destroyed.

Reznikoff wrote:

> Among the heaps of brick and plaster lies
> A girder, still itself among the rubbish.
> (published in *Poetry*, February 1931)

George Oppen credited this little poem with helping him survive combat and injury in World War Two.[41] Reznikoff's images, such as "the great chain" in the passage quoted above, consistently resist becoming symbols, just as the girder in these lines stubbornly remains "still itself." Nonetheless it is hard not to see Reznikoff's girder as Oppen clearly needed to, as an expression of a miraculous wholeness persisting intact amid the rubble of catastrophe. In the context of the Depression, when these lines were actually written, this image also must have had a particular power. I want to stress my point about how Reznikoff uses precise description and the accumulation of physical particulars to thwart the symbolist reflex before I turn to a consideration of *Testimony*'s final image, which contains one of the oldest and most freighted symbols in literary history, the mirror:

> As the case was turned over upon the wharf, a rattling was heard inside. The looking-glass was broken. The pieces were wedge-shaped; the cracks radiated from a center, as if the glass had been struck by a pointed instrument. (*Testimony* 3, "Depression," 4)

This is the last of the four passages comprising "Depression." The preceding sections are concerned, respectively, with insanity presumably brought on by money troubles, suicide (by stabbing and drowning) in response to financial ruin, and suicide by gunshot—suggesting a culture bent, ultimately, upon self-destruction. The last section stands out because it details an injury to an object rather than to a person. Whereas in the preceding sections the victim/perpetrator is identified (in each case by his full name), in the final passage the damage might have been deliberate or accidental, and no perpetrator is named. The image has been removed from its narrative context and purposefully isolated; any information that might help the reader determine the significance of this broken object has been withheld.

Reznikoff concludes *Testimony* with a speculative comment about the broken looking-glass: "the cracks radiated from the center, as if the glass had been struck by a pointed instrument." *Speculation* is a term originating in the image of the mirror (*speculum*), which has economic associations, as well: Reckless business speculation contributed to the crash of 1929. Most of the matter of *Testimony* consists of statements of fact—"fact" as defined within the contexts of the courtroom. By electing to conclude with an instance of guesswork rather than with a factual statement, Reznikoff shifts the discourse into a realm of uncertainty, a way of intentionally avoiding closure and leaving the work open-ended. Here, as elsewhere in *Testimony*, Reznikoff leaves it to the reader to examine the evidence and arrive at his or her own conclusions based on the information presented.

FORMS OF RESCUE

Michael Heller has written that "[i]n Reznikoff, the poem attains to the condition of the photograph rather than the lyric—the photograph, in the words of Walter Benjamin, as 'the posthumous moment,' the moment rescued from time."[42] With *Testimony*, Reznikoff began the construction of a complex and useful national history. As H. R. Hays wrote in his 1934 review of this work, "Certainly American history remains a thing to be created. The quantitative labors of scholars and the cheap-jingo-imagination of the schoolbooks have done no more than obscure it."[43] While *Testimony* invites readers to collaborate in the creation of alternative narratives, it reminds us there are non-narrative ways of making meaning, too. The past is present and physically recoverable in the materials of legal discourse, documentary records, letters, lists, textual images, prose, and poetry that Reznikoff mediates between in this text; the "deep vein of sympathy" Kenneth Burke correctly locates in Reznikoff's work brings to mind other senses of that term: mediation as intercession, a means of resolving conflict between parties, in order to promote reconciliation and bring about accord. With this in mind, we can finally revisit the epigraph to *Testimony* and find it free of irony: "Let all bitterness, and wrath, and anger, and clamour, and railing, be put away from you, with all malice." In *Testimony* Reznikoff discloses the potential, in our national past, for mutually sustaining communities that transverse socioeconomic and racial barriers. The evidence exists and may be retrieved, ironically enough, from within the records of humankind's inhumanity to itself.

Chapter Three

The Lyrical Apertures of George Oppen's *Discrete Series*

> Photography's modernist adventure might be described as a dialogue between the transparency of the open window and the impenetrable surface of the image.
>
> —Peter Galassi, in *Walker Evans & Company*

Discrete Series was published by the Objectivist Press in 1934, in a small edition George Oppen paid for himself. This slender volume of poems wrapped in a "light sea-green cloth binding"[1] featured a preface by Ezra Pound, and was reviewed in *Poetry* magazine by William Carlos Williams—two career-launching commendations for a young (Oppen was twenty-six) and relatively unknown poet. Another twenty-five years would pass before Oppen would publish another word.

Discrete Series begins *in medias res,* bringing the reader into the company of the speaker and an unidentified "you," resuming a conversation already in progress:

> The knowledge not of sorrow, you were
>   saying, but of boredom
> Is——aside from reading speaking
>   smoking——
> Of what, Maude Blessingbourne it was
>   wished to know when, having risen,
> "approached the window as if to see
>   what really was going on";
> And saw rain falling, in the distance
>   more slowly,

The road clear from her past the window-
    glass—
Of the world, weather-swept, with which
    one shares the century.
        (*New Collected Poems,* 5)

The single, complex sentence that comprises this poem delineates the terms of Oppen's commitment to a poetry based on empirical observation. A desire to see "what really was going on" and to construct a poetic object based on the conviction "that the nouns do refer to something; that it's there, that it's true,"[2] situates Oppen's work in direct relation to the documentary movement that flourished in the United States during the 1930s. Over the course of that decade, the camera ("the central instrument of our time," as James Agee proclaimed in 1936) turned viewers into eyewitnesses, exposing them to multiple images of contemporary American life. Oppen, along with Louis Zukofsky and Charles Reznikoff, anticipated the time's fascination with what Alfred Kazin called "the camera *as an idea.*"[3] Photography provided both Oppen and Reznikoff with a conceptual means for adapting certain Imagist principles, especially the belief that a poem should present rather than re-present, to their own purposes; they sought a poetic equivalent to the camera's ability to observe, without comment, and to directly present those observations to others.

UNMEDIATED VISION

Oppen, "the twentieth century master of camera eye vision," according to Harold Schimmel,[4] frequently used photographic and cinematic terms and analogies in discussions of his work. Oppen's poems consistently valorize the capacity of the "clear physical eye" (Zukofsky's phrase) to register each particular without distortion ("we have wanted / Not comforts / But vision"[5]). More than thirty years after the publication of *Discrete Series,* Oppen still reached instinctively for photographic metaphors, revealing the documentary affiliations of his work and his desire to "make poetry out of the clarity of the human vision"[6]:

> Words cannot be wholly transparent. And this is the 'heartlessness' of words. . . . More simply: the need to be able to shift focus, depth of focus, with precision, to control distance, real distance, I mean visual distance and audible distance and get at the crucial moments right on top of the thing, an inch from the thing: at that moment, no quotes, no references—at that moment, something near transparence after all—.[7]

"Something near transparence after all" expresses the longing for unmediated vision that haunts Oppen's poetry. His work aimed toward this objective, even as he acknowledged that one can never arrive at an experience of the world unmediated by language: "Words cannot be wholly transparent." Nonetheless, as the passage reveals, the effort to "get at the crucial moments right on top of the thing, an inch from the thing" might yield, on rare occasions, what Oppen called "clarity": the miraculous experience when "the real" may truly be seen and held, for a moment, in the mind.

The discussion cited above, from a 1966 letter, illustrates the fundamental contradiction in Oppen's poetry that I address in this chapter: how, in his pursuit of an unmediated vision of reality, Oppen persistently resorted to photographic metaphors—that is, metaphors of mechanical mediation—to describe that vision and the nature of his own poetics. Over the years, commentators, as well, have consistently used such figures in discussions of Oppen's work. I believe Oppen was aware of the presence of this contradiction in his poetry and that the poems in *Discrete Series* both explore and exploit it. Given the growing influence of the photographic medium in the United States and the extent to which social photography was widely trusted as a source of knowledge (more precisely, of truth) during the 1930s, I am intrigued by the idea that the American documentary movement was founded on a paradox related to the one I identify in Oppen's work. The most visible manifestation of the documentary impulse—the proliferation of documentary images in American newspapers and photo magazines—was also the least contested. In making the nation "real to itself," documentarians of the thirties relied on the fact that what smacked of propaganda in print became real and indisputable when presented in a photograph.

Correlations between *Discrete Series,* which Oppen called "very much an American poem, a poem of the thirties," and the documentary climate of that decade also help illuminate Oppen's conception of the poem as an object (hence the term "Objectivist") and the relationship of that verbal object to "reality"; these correlations point, as well, toward the surprising affiliations that exist between photography and poetry, affiliations which were thrown into relief by the exigencies of the time.

CONTEMPORARY PARTICULARS

As I argue in chapter 2 of this book ("Documentary Matters"), Charles Reznikoff's project in *Testimony* was to recover the materials of the American past and construct from them an alternative national narrative. If Reznikoff's focus in that text, published the same year as *Discrete Series,* was on the "historic

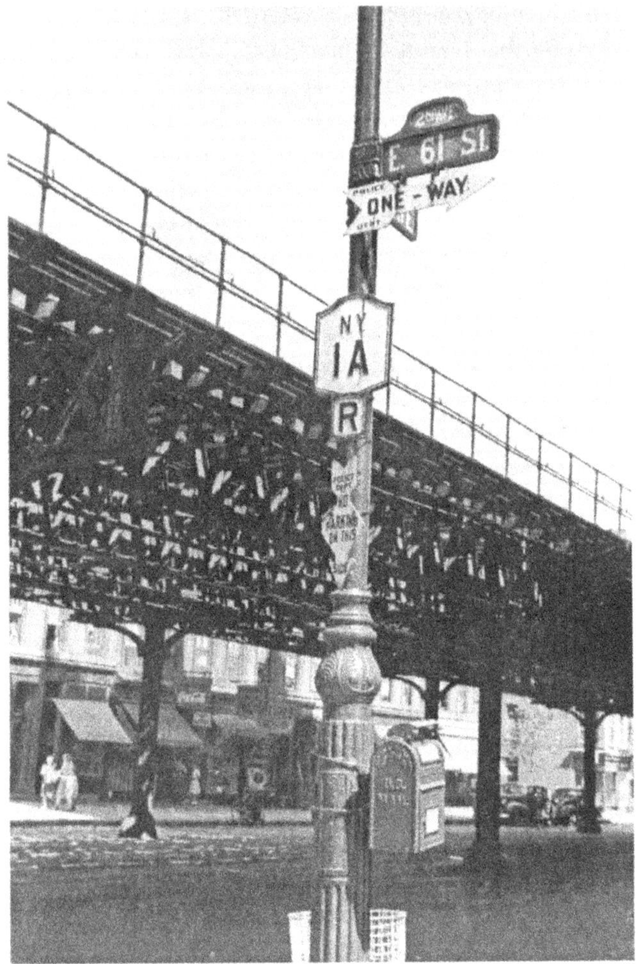

Fig. 3.1 Walker Evans. New York City, 61st Street between 1st and 3rd Avenues. View of street signs and the el train (Summer 1938)
Library of Congress, Prints and Photographs Division, LC-USF3301-006719-M1

particulars" that Zukofsky refers to in his essay "Program: 'Objectivists' 1931," Oppen was concerned with "contemporary particulars": what he witnessed taking place right before his eyes. What Oppen saw and wrote about "in Brooklyn, 1929" were his immediate surroundings: the streets and waterways of Red Hook and Manhattan; his wife, Mary; skyscrapers; tugboats; a string of laundry on a line. *Discrete Series* presents a succession of images from those years, constructed from language as concise and declarative as a black-and-white photograph:

Bad times:
The cars pass
By the elevated posts
And the movie sign.
A man sells post-cards.
(*NCP,* 30)

This particular scene feels deeply familiar to us, more than seventy years later, because we have seen it (or something close to it) in countless photographs of that time (see figure 3.1). Recalling those days, Oppen said, "I think it was fifteen million families that were faced with the threat of immediate starvation. It wasn't a business one simply read about in the newspaper. You stepped out your door and found men who had nothing to eat."[8] As in Reznikoff's verse, the poet's job in a piece like "Bad times" is comparable to that of the photographer: He is intent on seeing and on not being seen. The poet's "lens" isolates and frames a momentary and random intersection of objects and events and fixes that image in the emulsion of language. And like Reznikoff, Oppen crafts his concise lyrics using flat, monochromatic diction to present, without overt commentary, scenes from ordinary life. However, Oppen achieves a substantially different effect. Whereas Reznikoff's images often seem suffused with a sympathy that emanates from the rhythms and tonal qualities of the language, Oppen's poems are often purposefully atonal, refusing the fluencies available in the language.

In "Bad times" the repetition of "posts" and "post-cards" may seem artless at first, until one notices how the reiteration of certain sounds in these brief lines (pass-posts-post-cards / movie-man / signs-sells / cars-cards) slyly declares the poem's status as a carefully crafted verbal object. The "flatness" of Oppen's language is the flatness of a two-dimensional surface, and try as we might to simply look through these words at the scene they describe, the poem prevents us from doing so. Brian Reed describes how, in *Discrete Series,* "[t]he words obstruct unmediated access to the thing portrayed. They redirect our attention towards language's own status as a concrete object to be manipulated."[9] How else is this redirection accomplished? The particulars that Oppen focuses on in "Bad times" (a man, cars, the el tracks, a movie marquee) are highly generalized and the details left to the reader's imagination. Here Oppen's precision emerges not in his descriptions of individual things (since he hardly describes at all) but in the care with which he delineates the relationships between these objects, visually (the way the words look on the page), syntactically, and aurally, using patterns of sound. The results Oppen achieves with these techniques are purposefully ambivalent: "Bad times" hovers somewhere between transparence and opacity, mediating between language that refers to something beyond itself (i.e., "the world") and language that points back to itself as a medium. This double effect, achieved subtly in "Bad times," is characteristic of all the poems in *Discrete Series.*

MECHANICS AND MACHINES

In their respective responses to *Discrete Series,* both Pound and Williams use metaphors that depict poetry as a form of manual labor. Defending Oppen against the charge that he writes like Williams (he really doesn't; I examine some of the differences between these poets in chapter 4), Pound concludes his "Preface" by declaring: "I salute a serious craftsman, a sensibility which is not every man's sensibility and which has not been got out of any other man's books" (*NCP,* 4). In his review of *Discrete Series,* which appeared in *Poetry* magazine, Williams describes Oppen as a type of mechanical engineer:

> Oppen has moved to present a clear outline for an understanding of what a new construction should require. His poems seek an irreducible minimum in the means for the achievement of their objective, no loose bolts or beams sticking out unattached at one end and put there to hold up a rococo cupid or a concrete saint . . . This is the work of a "stinking" intellectual, if you please. That is, you should use the man as you would use any other mechanic—to serve a purpose for which training, his head, his general abilities fit him, to build with—that others may build after him.[10]

Williams used this review as a platform to air some of his own theories and do a little sniping at his old pal Pound. His title, "The New Poetical Economy," also points toward Pound, whose insistence upon verbal economy was expressed in the Imagist dictum: "To use absolutely no word that does not contribute to the presentation." Oppen by no means served as a dutiful apprentice to either poet; he had his own ideas about how poems are made, as he effectively demonstrates in *Discrete Series.*

Williams's famous definition of the poem as "a small (or large) machine made of words" would not appear in print until a decade later (in *The Wedge,* 1944), but his review of *Discrete Series* proves that he had formulated these ideas previously, maybe even in response to Oppen's text. The era's preoccupation with machine forms is certainly evident in *Discrete Series.* Encountering these poems, one is struck by how many include images of machines and different kinds of mechanical processes. The work presents an industrial landscape, paved over and cluttered with mechanical devices: an elevator, a refrigerator and soda fountain, tugboats, ships, sailboats, steamshovels and steamrollers, artificial lights, cars and limousines, various kinds of trains, streetcars, and, finally, the telephone. However, the machine that implicitly dominates *Discrete Series* and its perspectives never actually appears in these poems, except indirectly: "Civil war photo: / Grass near the lens" (*NCP,* 21). Associated with the "I," the camera eye stays out of sight.

MODERN TECHNOLOGIES

A new kind of vision, one distinctly modern in sensibility and documentary in intent, demands new poetic forms as well as a new critical approach. In the 1934 edition of *Discrete Series,* the text was laid out one poem to a page, making the arrangement of white space an essential element in the presentation. The prefatory poem ("The knowledge not of sorrow") appeared on a verso, facing a blank page, suggesting that the stage has been swept clean ("weather-swept") for what follows. The involuted syntax of the proem, with its conversational tone, does little to challenge our formal expectations. Any comfort the reader may have taken in this familiarity is stripped away when the page is turned:

1

White. From the
Under arm of T

The red globe.

Up
Down. Round
Shiny fixed
Alternatives

From the quiet

Stone floor . . .
(*NCP,* 6)

Obvious differences exist between this poem and "The knowledge not of sorrow," not to mention most poetry being published during that those years ("If you look at the anthologies of the time, you'll see it was avant garde alright").[11] When this poem initially appeared in Louis Zukofsky's *An "Objectivists" Anthology* (1932), it was entitled "1930'S [sic]," which situates both its subject matter and its method within a specific historical context.

"White" imprints itself on the mind's eye as a sequence of perceptual fragments regulated by white space: *red, up, down, round, shiny*—the isolated visual impressions a baby might absorb or the first words in a child's reader, identifying the basic qualities and relationships that enable us to locate ourselves in the world and in relation to the things around us. The first word (really, the first "sentence," since it is followed by a period) confronts us with the ambiguity of blankness: White can be a void, or like white light, may contain all colors of the spectrum. By creating such a field of hermeneutic possibilities, Oppen makes unfamiliar demands on the reader. He constructs this poem from isolated words and sentence fragments that present seemingly abstract patterns of color and movement. He forces us to dwell on the individual textual components—that is, on the poem's "surface," its two-dimensionality—before we can grasp what its components refer to in the world beyond that surface. Then the subject matter of "White" suddenly becomes clear to us, in a flash of recognition.

Years later, Oppen would acknowledge that "the poems require the help, the great good will of the reader."[12] Not everyone was willing to do this work: An early review of *Discrete Series* was downright hostile, dismissing Oppen's images as "anti-poems" born not of a poetic womb, but of "an isolated dried-up bladder."[13] This reviewer fails to notice that these brief, challenging pieces are often charged with emotion and even sensuality. In the poetic Rorschach blot of "White" critics have discovered images as various as a child bouncing a ball (Tomlinson)[14], a female nude (Schimmel), and a milk-dispensing machine (Chilton).[15] The immediate reference for the poem has been lost in time; however baffled they may have been by its other devices, Oppen's contemporaries presumably would have recognized these visual cues as constituting an image of an elevator, an interpretation supported by the prepositions "up" and "down" as well as other clues in the poem. (A familiar ornamental device over elevator doors in the thirties featured a T-shaped crossbar with lighted globes to indicate the direction of the car's progress.) Oppen's emergence as a poet coincided with the period of the 1929 stock market crash, an economic free fall that erased fortunes overnight. *Discrete Series* reflects the time's concern with these "Shiny fixed/Alternatives," and suggests, as well, the new vocabulary and metaphors that contemporary technologies made available to describe those events.

YOU ARE A CAMERA

The various interpretations of "White" cited above, although wide of the mark in one sense, seem to gesture toward the mysterious interpenetration of the human and the mechanical that characterizes so many of the poems in *Discrete Series.* More than a decade earlier, surveying the revolutionary changes that occurred in the decade between 1912–1922 and their impact on literature, the French critic Jean Epstein wrote:

> The machine technology of civilization . . . allows man an infinite variety of angles of observation. Optics especially—and what is there astonishing in this, in a civilization which is essentially optical—hangs its lenses round our necks like the amulets on the neck of an Indian chief. All these instruments . . . are not merely dead objects. At certain times these machines become part of ourselves, interposing themselves between the world and us, filtering reality as the screen filters radium emanations. Thanks to them, we have no longer a simple, clear, continuous, constant notion of an object.[16]

Two perceptual changes are especially worth noting here: first, Epstein's description of the ways in which new technologies help disclose novel views of reality (the view of Paris from the top of the Eiffel Tower, for instance); and second, how these instruments designed to extend the senses actually become a part of us, blurring the distinctions between a tool and the person who wields it. Instruments, machines, technical apparatuses have become coextensive with our bodies in this latest stage of human evolution.

I think Epstein makes a logical error, however, when he equates this merging with mediation: "[A]t certain times these machines become part of ourselves, interposing themselves between the world and us, filtering reality as a screen filters radium emanations." To begin with, machines cannot interpose themselves anywhere (at least, not yet); it is human beings who put them to use. I see this blending of the mechanical and the human as part of Oppen's response to the problem of mediation that the poems explore. As mass-produced images became ubiquitous in American culture they also became naturalized, so that people stopped regarding them as constructions and instead came to accept them as extensions of their own perceptions. As the mechanism of the camera merged with human vision, it ceased to be recognized as a medium; it was no longer interposed "between the world and us" because, suddenly, it *was* us.

We have grown accustomed to this evolutionary development: Look how casually we accept the incredible journeys the eye takes daily. When we look at still photographs or watch films our eyes travel to the bottom of the ocean, over the rocky Martian surface, past the shoulder of a goose in flight, into the core of an electronic particle. We accept these marvels without a flicker of astonishment because we take for granted the technology that carries our eyes to all those places. Our vision knows no limits, and yet that fact has lost the power to amaze us. We don't notice the medium anymore that constructs our views of reality.

Epstein's essay shows that this process was well underway when Oppen began work on *Discrete Series* at the end of the 1920s. In his pursuit of new poetic forms to express the changing environment, Oppen explored new ways of relating to machines—not only in the images of machines his poems include, but also in the forms of the poems and the literary devices they employ. His work seems very much of a piece with contemporaneous intellectual debates regarding technology's role in human civilization.

The year *Discrete Series* appeared also saw the publication of Lewis Mumford's *Technics and Civilization* (1934). In this monumental book, Mumford (1895–1990) argues that technology (what Mumford called "technics") had reached a stage where "the organic has become visible again." He credits the innovations of the "neotechnic" age, including the motion picture, telegraph, telephone, phonograph, and radio, with restoring the human eye, ear, and voice to the mechanized world. Science and mechanization do not threaten human culture; rather, they enable it, and Mumford contends that

> our capacity to go beyond the machine rests upon our power to assimilate the machine. Until we have absorbed the lessons of objectivity, impersonality, neutrality, the lessons of the mechanical realm, we cannot go further in our development toward the more richly organic, the more profoundly human.[17]

The proper harnessing of technology, according to Mumford, also creates "new" aesthetic terms such as "precision, calculation, flawlessness, simplicity, economy . . . elimination of the non-essential"[18]—all qualities celebrated by Pound and others decades earlier, of course. In his later works (such as *The Myth of the Machine,* 1964), Mumford would espouse a far more distopian view of the effects of technology on human culture.

By citing Mumford's "neotechnic" theories I do not wish to imply that Oppen subscribed to them, but he must have been familiar with Mumford's work—especially since his own book and Mumford's were both reviewed in the final issue of *Hound & Horn* (July–September 1934). (The ultimate issue of this literary quarterly features a favorable review of *Technics and Civilization* as well as a piece by H. R. Hays entitled "Nothing But the Truth," which looks briefly at *Discrete Series* and other books published by the Objectivist Press that year.) Nor do I intend to suggest that Oppen's view of mechanization was similarly optimistic. As I will show, several poems in *Discrete Series* address the negative aspects of these encroaching technologies and the ways in which they distort our perceptions, and most demonstrate a distinct ambivalence toward machine processes. The poem "White," reproduced above, objectifies this ambivalence in the alternative motions of the elevator (up and down), the contradictory phrase "fixed / Alternatives," and the sepulchral connotations of the "quiet / Stone floor . . ."

Still, it must have come naturally to Oppen, who eventually became a machinist and a skilled carpenter, to see tools as extensions of the tool user. One detects a certain pride in Oppen's references to his own mechanical abilities (in his correspondence, for example), which may stem, in part, from his fulfillment of that romantic scenario common in the thirties: the rich kid who rejects his own social class to affiliate himself with the workers. *Discrete Series* is a virtuoso display of Oppen's technical abilities, particularly his skill at manipulating the "camera eye." A cinematic analogy is especially appropriate to characterize Oppen's methods in these poems, which include techniques of lighting, angles of vision, close-ups, and framing. Coincidentally, D. W. Griffith lived next door to Oppen's family in New Rochelle, New York:

> They may never have met, though the child later mastered and adapted certain of the director's techniques: the *close-up* and the *iris*, the isolation of the particular in the panorama of history or of a culture; and *parallel cutting*, the story or poem projected forward through the elimination of transitions, a meaningful blank space between the shots of lines, the play and act of redefinition that occur through the juxtaposition of similar or opposite images.[19]

For a time, Oppen's father operated a string of movie houses.

PHOTOMONTAGE

By focusing our attention on certain components of the urban interior in "White" (via the nouns, and the definite articles that point to them, as well as by the line breaks), Oppen not only directs the mind's eye in a manner that recreates the physical eye's saccadic motions as it might take in the particulars of the scene in life,[20] but he imitates the motions of a movie camera, alternately panning and zeroing in on discrete visual elements. Oppen once remarked in an interview that the focus of *Discrete Series* jumps around "like the fashionable camera of that time,"[21] and the series does resemble a photomontage, spliced together from linguistic pieces pared down to their essentials, all transitions and expositions eliminated. Montage makes meaning via visual proximity, and creates relationships simply by putting one thing next to another. Simultaneously, the shifting eye of the reader gathering its motes of information from the page has been directed swiftly downward by the import of the words themselves (*Stone floor,* and descendental words of foundation or origin: *from, under*) as well as by the fact that the English page is read in this direction. Situating us within the architectural form most emblematic of modernism, a form that strives (despite the alternatives of ascent and descent it encloses) resolutely upward, Oppen leads our perceptions in the opposite direction.

METAPHOR AND METONYMY

Oppen generally avoids metaphor in his poetry; when he does utilize this device, he employs it in unconventional ways. Objectivist poetry is centrifugal in nature, tending outward in its perceptions rather than concentrating inward on the source of those perceptions in the mind of the poet, a kind of "other-centeredness" that is also one of the earmarks of documentary photography. In contrast, conventional metaphors focus attention on the metaphor-maker, whose tropes, as Oppen once said, "can scarcely have been part of the poet's attempt to find himself in the world."[22] He rejects such metaphors because they put the poet's inventiveness on display. Metaphor also shifts attention, at least momentarily, away from the original object; it moves our minds elsewhere, from the tenor to the vehicle.

In "The Love Song of J. Alfred Prufrock," T. S. Eliot's famous synecdoche "I should have been a pair of ragged claws" functions as an objective correlative for the psychic state of Prufrock, Eliot's persona in the poem. Oppen's elevator in the poem beginning "White," in comparison, serves no such motive. It functions as a synecdoche of itself, assembling in our minds just as the other details that Oppen provides evoke, in the dynamic mysteries of their relations to one another, the image of a skyscraper. Oppen works within a discourse based upon contiguity rather than similarly, favoring metonymy over metaphor because the former offers a means of exploring the relationships between part and whole, particular and universal, as well as between poet and reader. Oppen's preference for metonymy over metaphor is appropriate for a documentary poetic, since one of the crucial functions of the documentary image is to relate the part to the whole, to establish the singular reality of the subject while simultaneously revealing its universality and thus its connection with the viewer.

SEEING LESSONS

Reading "White" teaches us what we need to know in order to encounter the poem on the facing page. In this respect, the poem functions as a primer of Objectivist seeing. Oppen's elevator, emerging out of the metonymic tensions between part and whole, between what the poet's "lens" selects and what we must recover on the basis of those details, prepares us for the machinery of concealment at work in the poem on the facing page:

2

  Thus
Hides the

Parts—the prudery
Of Frigidaire, of
Soda-jerking—

Thus

Above the

Plane of lunch, of wives
Removes itself
(As soda-jerking from
the private act

Of
Cracking eggs);

big-Business
  (*NCP,* 7)

"White" and "Thus," numbered 1 and 2, respectively, represent a new beginning within the larger series. Each poem is arranged in a narrow column on the page and features short lines interspersed with white space. Unexpected line breaks call attention to the little words that don't usually attract much notice: *the, from, of.* The subject matter of these poems is also complementary, since each presents a feature of modern urban architecture.

Discussions of "Thus" often remark on Oppen's critique of capitalism.[23] The thirties witnessed the continuing expansion of this new economic power, monolithic and faceless as the structures it erected, which Oppen depicts as concealing its dubious machinations behind glossy surfaces and advertising campaigns ("Thus / Hides the / Parts"), far above the oblivious heads bent over lunch counters. As a budding Marxist, Oppen surely regarded the rise of the corporate state with concern. Full of syntactical evasions, the poem seems to slither backward, and persistently away from, its ultimate disclosure. The strange formality of the word "Thus," repeated in the sixth line, along with the recurring preposition "of" (five times in a 30-word poem), gesture vaguely toward an explanation, a cause or a source, which is withheld until the poem's final line.

Less has been written about the sexual overtones of this piece: the implications of shame and nudity ("Hides the / Parts"), masturbation ("soda-jerking"), and illicit gropes behind office doors. Oppen's pun on the brand name in the lines "the prudery / Of Frigidaire" equates the chilly demeanor of repressed sexuality with the polished exteriors of the new commodities. Oppen's working papers contain a suggestive gloss on the poem:

> To masturbate is to convince oneself that a cushion is a pretty girl.
> To masturbate is to call a pretty girl—anything else but that. Or to call the desire to be loved back—anything more or less than that.
> To inflate or treat with contempt—is onanism.
> So is fancy language.
> And 'the prudery
> Of Frigidaire'[24]

As Lisa Steinman points out in her study of the influence of science and technology on modern American poetry, modernist poets sought to masculinize their art, which the American public regarded as effeminate, by relating it via machine aesthetics to the supposed "virility" of business and industry.[25] Oppen, however, uses industrial imagery in this poem to undermine the equation of gender and technology by exposing its questionable practices and by suggesting how it commodifies women ("Of lunch, of wives"). The only pronoun in the poem ("itself") is, appropriately, neutered and reflexive. Here the blending of human and machine has unequivocally negative connotations.

From a documentary standpoint, then, Oppen presents an image of his time that sketches, in a few lines, not only the character of its economic, architectural, and rhetorical structures and the interrelationships between them, but which also suggests some of its dubious sexual politics. By such means is the reader made aware of the world beyond the poem, and also of the poem itself as constituting a precise and ongoing historical moment.

The axis of investigation here is at once vertical and horizontal, and we seem to witness activities on these different planes occurring simultaneously. The overall effect is something akin to X-ray vision: Oppen's image objectifies the act of seeing, which is also the act of seeing through, or insight, piercing through false and distracting façades. The original gesture of looking out a window, valorized in the proem to *Discrete Series,* is thus revisited, with significant variations, throughout the text. Moreover, the whole notion of what constitutes vision has been radically complicated, which may help explain some of the bafflement and hostility that greeted this work in 1934. (Oppen dramatized the work's initial reception in his notes: "Oppen: Look out the window. The public: Window? Out?"[26]) These complications define the parameters of Oppen's documentary vision, the paradoxical means of achieving "clarity" in his poetry. The window-glass that Maude Blessingbourne looks through, an aperture allowing only limited access since it also represents a barrier between the seer and "the world, weather-swept," reoccurs in a series of reflective surfaces: in the glass globes of the elevator mechanism, the polished lunch counter, the gleaming chrome of appliances and automobiles, but also in a ship's porthole, "the glass of windows," the surface of a limousine window—and the camera lens.

THE PASSIONATE MECHANIC

> Automobiles, and the automobile landscape. Architecture, American urban taste, commerce, small scale, large scale, the city street atmosphere . . .
> The movies.
> —Walker Evans's notes for shooting subjects, from a 1934 letter

Another image of Oppen's ambivalence regarding mechanization and technology occurs in the third poem in the series:

> The evening, water in a glass
> Thru which our car runs on a higher road.
>
> Over what has the air frozen?

Nothing can equal in polish and obscured
    origin that dark instrument
A car
        (Which.
Ease; the hand on the sword-hilt
                    (*NCP,* 8)

A note among Oppen's working papers offered this elaboration upon Williams's well-known definition: "a poem is a machine made of words to carry the poet to where he is going"[27]—and quickly, he might have added. This notion of the poem as a means of transportation, a streamlined medium of communication, may partially explain the recurring images of cars and other vehicles in *Discrete Series.* The twentieth-century preoccupation with speed is evident in the minimalist forms of these poems and the telegraphic shorthand of their dispatches. Oppen conveys the simultaneously seductive and sinister quality of "that dark instrument / A car" with the economy of contemporary advertising copy—in fact, the poem reads like the shooting script for a Lexus commercial. In the course of a conversation about his poem "Image of the Engine" (1962), Oppen once told L. S. Dembo, "I am a fairly passionate mechanic,"[28] and it shows.

Who comes is occupied
Toward the chest (in the crowd moving
        opposite
Grasp of me)
            In firm overalls
The middle-aged man sliding
Levers in the steam-shovel cab,—
Lift (running cable) and swung, back
Remotely respond to the gesture before last
Of his arms fingers continually—
Turned with the cab. But if I (how goes
        it?)—
                The asphalt edge
Loose on the plateau,
Horse's classic height cartless
See electric flash of streetcar,
The fall is falling from electric burst.
                (*NCP,* 14)

This is a difficult poem to gloss and, ultimately, perhaps not a wholly successful one (Oppen himself admitted as much). However, it presents a handy example of the process I am investigating, in its image of successive technologies superimposed on the raw land ("the plateau") underneath the asphalt. The way the steam-shovel operator's motions are translated by his machinery into an entirely new (though intimately related) series of movements is, linguistically speaking, a technical achievement in itself. "Who comes" is also a marvelous demonstration of the operations of the Objectivist poem. Again, these poems create a mental impression of vision occurring on several levels at once, and the impressions they conjure up before the mind's eye are not images in any straightforward or conventional sense.

OPPEN AND HENRY JAMES

The character of Maud Blessingbourne, along with a fragment of text appropriated from Henry James's "The Story in It" (1902), furnished Oppen with the central image of *Discrete Series,* an image embodying the visual imperative that the poem serially reenacts. For this reason, I want to revisit this prefatory piece before resuming my commentary on the remaining poems in the series. Discussing *Discrete Series* in a 1969 interview with L. S. Dembo, Oppen confessed: "I wanted James in the book—secretly, superstitiously, I carved his initials on that sapling book. . . ."[29] Oppen's evocation of James's sentence structure in "The knowledge not of sorrow" was a means of breathing that writer's spirit into the sails of his text.[30] Along with Flaubert and Stendhal, James was among the writers known for their precise empirical observations and psychological realism that Pound cited as exemplars for the poets of his generation. James's character Maud (Oppen gives her an extra e—Maude) Blessingbourne is a product of the nineteenth century; her surname alone conjures up a world of social privilege that must be, in Marxian terms, consigned to the dustbin of history. (Is there a hint of the new broom in Oppen's adjective "weather-swept"?) For Oppen, who only belatedly managed to free himself from the safety net of his own upper-class background, a rejection of this class structure amounted to both an ethical stance and a political necessity.

Oppen's complex syntax offers the reader a number of interpretive possibilities, one of which might be elided "The knowledge, not of sorrow, you were saying, but of boredom / Is . . . / Of what, Maude Blessingbourne . . . wished to know when, having risen, / approached the window as if to see what really was going on." Oppen has inverted James's wording—originally "what was really going on"—to emphasize the root of the adverb, "real." (Referring to this line in a letter, Oppen supplied commas for emphasis: "to know what, really, was going on."[31]) Oppen continues the sentence beyond the quotation marks after the break of the semicolon: "And saw rain falling, in the distance / more slowly, /The road clear from her past the window-/ glass—" The sentence straightens and extends itself (with the help of Oppen's characteristic extra-long dash), gaining momentum for the elegant phrasing of the poem's final lines.

This initial poem is intentionally set off from those that follow. The phrasing of that last line, as Harold Schimmel has said, is "gorgeous," and self-consciously so. In his study of *Discrete Series,* Tom Sharp notes how Maude functions here to illustrate a specific philosophical concept, which can be stated as "The knowledge of the mood of boredom is the knowledge of the world."[32] Sharp points out that "To state the concept is to break the discipline which is maintained in the thirty subsequent poems, which present, without comment, the Image encountered in the concrete experience."[33] By positioning this poem at the entrance to the series, Oppen effectively declares his independence from the narrative conventions extant in that text.

HEIDEGGER'S BOREDOM

In a 1967 letter, Oppen reflected upon his use of Heidegger's word "boredom":

> . . . the first poem in Discrete Series . . . was written in 1929. That, I've learned, was the year in which H. was giving his Inauguration Speech in which he spoke of the mood of boredom which leads . . . to "the knowledge of what-is."[34]

In his correspondence, Oppen acknowledges the German philosopher's ideas and their influence upon his work. Regarding the prefatory poem in the series, Oppen explained: "Heidegger's statement that in the mood of boredom the existence of what-is is disclosed, is my Maude Blessingbourne in *Discrete Series* who in 'boredom' looks out the window and sees 'the world/ weather-swept, with which/one shares the century.'"[35] Heidegger's term does not refer to a specific response to something that bores us, but rather to a generalized mood (what he calls "profound boredom") that can render one receptive to the knowledge of Being, the "what-is." (Similarly, a generalized sense of joy or anxiety may also open one's consciousness to this pure manifestation of being.) In Oppen's poetics, where truth arises from the encounter between the perceiver and the object of perception, one's emotional response to the real—a response consistently presented in the form of a complex image—actually constitutes its truth, the sudden upsurge of felt existence that Oppen called "awe."

Discussing his method in these poems, Oppen described it as "that Heideggerian gesture of pointing"[36]: "[T]he poems have that quality of simply pointing at the thing as a way of constructing a poem."[37] Later in the series, the poems gesture toward these local scenes:

> The edge of the ocean,
> The shore: here
> Somebody's lawn,
> By the water.
> (*NCP,* 18)

> Tug against the river—
> Motor turning, lights
> In the fast water off the bow-wave:
> Passes slowly.
> (*NCP,* 19)

To point at something is to locate it in space, to direct another's attention to something specific, to help them look at and perhaps see it. Therefore, pointing is essentially a documentary gesture, and the indicative the basic documentary mood. In *Discrete Series* this gesture is accomplished in various ways: via words that indicate, such as the noun "here," the direct article "the," and the pronoun "this"; typographically, by using white space, extra-long dashes, line breaks, and punctuation to isolate words and direct attention; by using nouns in the absence of verbs and predicates; by avoiding the first-person pronoun and favoring the second-person; and by repeated images that picture vision and the act of looking. The initial image of looking out ("The road clear from her past the window- / glass—") in the proem initiates this gesture, indicating all the instances of pointing that follow. By making this poem a preface to the series as a whole, Oppen's foregrounds a documentary approach in *Discrete Series.*

OUT THERE IS THE WORLD

By its conclusion, this poem redirects its focus, and that of the reader, out into "the world, weather-swept, with which / one shares the century." Inevitably, the path of vision/knowledge extends into what Oppen referred to as "the direction outward, the miraculous dimension"[38] and downward, seeking fundamental contact with the "out-there."

The impulse to journey outward in pursuit of knowledge was not merely a poetic gesture on Oppen's part. A desire to "see what was really going on" prompted Oppen and Mary Colby to travel throughout the United States and later to France, in order to find out—as Mary said, echoing Sherwood Anderson—"if [they] were any good out there."[39] These two continuously put their principles and convictions to the test, in their writing and their lives. During 1928–1929, years when George was crafting the poems in *Discrete Series,* he and Mary hitchhiked around the country. In her autobiography *Meaning a Life,* Mary Oppen describes their wanderings and the knowledge they sought in their travels. In the spring of 1933, they returned to the United States from France, along with other Americans retreating from an economically depressed Europe, to rediscover their own country: "We were in search of an esthetic within which to live, and we were looking for it in our American roots, in our own country," Mary wrote.[40] Like growing numbers of itinerant social photographers and reporters who traveled around documenting what they found, the Oppens wanted to experience America firsthand and to record these discoveries in their work. In *Meaning a Life* many of the images of New York in the thirties call to mind documentary photographs of the period: "As we approached the first stoplight, grown men, respectable men—our fathers—stepped forward to ask for a nickel, rag in hand to wipe our windshield."[41] One still witnesses the same scene in most major American cities. Apparently not much has changed since then, except the value of a nickel and what people think of as noteworthy.

In his life and writing, Oppen sought to construct an epistemology based on documentary evidence ("The thing / By which the mind / Sees!" [*NCP,* 294]) and empirically derived truths. The proem to *Discrete Series* initiates the transition from a nineteenth-century Eurocentric perspective to a twentieth-century, distinctively American way of seeing in its shift from past into present tense; the thirty remaining poems all occur in the present.

"THE POEM AS LENS"

Hugh Kenner remarked on the documentary context of Objectivist poetics in his 1982 essay, "Oppen, Zukofsky, and the Poem as Lens": "As the first great decade of social photography opened, the decade of Dorothea Lange, Walker Evans, Margaret Bourke-White, the poem was directed to work, with leisured sophistication, like the photograph."[42] Taking his cue from Zukofsky's figure of the Objectivist poem as "The lens bringing the rays from an object to a focus," Kenner argues that the proper analogy for how the Objectivist poem works is "not the photograph but the photographic process itself, recreated in slow motion."[43] Nonetheless, Kenner's examples seem to undermine this distinction, since he persistently directs our attention to the poems' appearance and uses descriptive terms appropriate to still photography. Kenner calls Zukofsky's poem "To my washstand" a "sharp-focus monochromatic study," and says "We can imagine all that in a fine glossy black-and-white eight-by-ten."[44] In *Discrete Series* Kenner calls attention to the way in which "the poems go by like snapshots in an album."[45]

EMOTION AND VISION

I agree with Kenner that many of the poems in *Discrete Series* give us glimpses of a new photographic sensibility characteristic of the thirties—stark, hard-edged, and streamlined—the kind of sharply defined poetic contours ("hard-edgedness") that Pound had called for in his Imagist manifesti more than a decade earlier. However, Kenner fails to note the relationship between vision and emotion in Oppen's poetics. Kenner describes the operations of an Objectivist poem as if it were a kind of affectless (i.e., "objective"), automatic process: "Through the lens stream photons responsive to the randomness of the physical world, the world that is simply *there.*"[46] For Oppen, the fact that the world "is simply there," leaving proofs of its presence in the emulsion of the photographic plate and within the consciousness of the poet, is a recurring cause for wonder. As Oppen insists in "World, World——": "The self is no mystery, the mystery is / That there is something for us to stand on" (*NCP,* 159). For Oppen, seeing things intensely leads to moments of conviction when one can grasp that what is "out there" actually does exist. This experience amounts to a secular revelation, equivalent to that Heideggerian moment when truth discloses itself. Such moments occur in Oppen's later poetry (see "Psalm," for instance), but are by no means absent from *Discrete Series.* The passivity that Kenner attributes to the Objectivist poetic procedure seems an inaccurate description of an image alive with these kinds of energies:

> The mast
> Inaudibly soars; bole-like, tapering:
> Sail flattens from it beneath the wind.
> The limp water holds the boat's round
> sides. Sun
> Slants dry light on the deck.
> Beneath us glide
> Rocks, sand, and unrimmed holes.
> (*NCP,* 12)

A version of the relationship between vision and emotion at the core of Oppen's work can also be found in the documentary expression of the 1930s. The documentary impulse arises from a complex of desires (among them, the desire to witness, to investigate, to understand, to alter reality); there is nothing neutral or passive about the motivation to document a thing, or an event, and this inevitably biases how the thing itself is documented. In *Documentary Expression and Thirties America,* William Stott writes that "in thirties' documentary as a whole, feeling comes first."[47] The British producer and filmmaker John Grierson was well aware of the relationship between documentary and emotion: "I look to register what actually moves: what hits the spectator at the midriff; what yanks him up by the hair of the head or the plain bootstraps to the plane of decent seeing."[48] However, the capacity of images to elicit an emotional response from the viewer was something documentary makers often pressed to sentimental or propagandistic advantage: " . . . one knows another's life because one feels it; one is informed—one sees—through one's feelings. The practitioners of the documentary genre in the thirties realized, if dimly, the same thing: emotion counted more than fact."[49]

Poetry that regards the things of the world with a lyrical eye may slip into sentimentality, one of the lurking risks of realism. Oppen recognized this danger and actively fought against it by maintaining a neutrality of tone and by crafting his images with extreme precision and accuracy. Minimalism, "the new poetical economy," guards against sentimentality by eliminating the redundancies associated with emotional excess. In Oppen's work sincerity amounts to a poetic discipline that guards against the temptation to sentimentalize. As Michael Heller explains:

> [If] Objectivist "sincerity" means anything, it is not there simply to imply authentic connection with what is being said or with accurate rendition. Rather, sincerity . . . is a bearing, a grace under pressure of alternative, consoling, imaginative schemes. What is meant to convince about Objectivist poetry is its sense of having been created within, as Zukofsky states, a "context based on the world."[50]

Like the Objectivist poem, the most successful documentary photographs objectify the act of attending to a particular subject and seeking to grasp its truth through emotional means. In his description of the Image, Pound speaks about "that sense of sudden growth, which we experience in the presence of the greatest works of art."[51] Photographs frequently provoke this kind of immediate emotional response from the viewer; in Heidegger's terms, the viewer experiences this flash of disclosure when the perceptual becomes the conceptual, the particular expands into the universal. Oppen sought to construct a poetic image that would elicit the same sort of emotional response on the part of the reader. Such a response actually constitutes the truth that the poem discloses.

THE IMAGE AS A PROOF

In employing analogies drawn from documentary photography and film, both Kenner and Alan Golding overlook the essential contradiction at the heart of the documentary poetics of Objectivism: If the poet's objective is to construct a verbal object that provides an opportunity for unmediated access to actuality, "the pure joy / Of the mineral fact" (*NCP,* 164), why describe the operations of that poem in photographic terms, since the camera is an instrument of mediation and therefore a barrier to direct contact?

In a letter to Donald Davie in which Oppen discusses his poetic method, he declared that "my 'proofs' are all images. My proof is the image."[52] A photographic proof is, of course, a print made from an exposed and developed negative; it presents evidence of the impenetrable matter of the world that leaves its mark in the film's emulsion. The photographic image qualifies, semantically speaking, as a "trace": proof that such a thing as "reality" really exists. Oppen's poetic image functions as a test or proof of his sincerity: If his image is authentic, it will successfully embody a particular truth ("That which one cannot / Not see" [*NCP,* 185]) that may be communicated to the reader. The verbal object that is the Objectivist poem also qualifies as a trace, then, since the fact of its existence is a record of something indisputably real, as far as Oppen is concerned. As William Stott points out, the testimony of documentary evidence is unarguable.[53] Oppen's image-as-proof amounts to a kind of documentary evidence available to the reader, and the testimony it presents cannot be refuted or denied. Documentary photography and Oppen's documentary poetic, admittedly two very different forms of expression, thus strive in complementary respects toward a shared objective: a way of seeing that enables another (a viewer / a reader) to emotionally grasp a particular, irrefutable truth about the world.

DEGREES OF REALITY

If the real is the most positively valorized quality in Oppen's work, the false or the unreal represents its negative counterpart. Oppen's populism is most evident when he writes about degrees of reality: For him, some things are more real than others. One finds this notion alive in the rhetoric as well as in the documentary expression of the time (and even now people talk about "keeping it real"), and it is essentially a class distinction, since the most "real" people inevitably belong to the working class. The most negative objects presented in *Discrete Series* are those associated with falseness and wealth.

> Closed car—closed in glass—
> At the curb,
> Unapplied and empty:
> A thing among others
> Over which clouds pass and the
>   alteration of lighting,
> An overstatement
> Hardly an exterior.
> Moving in traffic
> This thing is less strange—
> Tho the face, still within it,
> Between glasses—place, over which
>   time passes—a false light.
>   (*NCP,* 13)

In an interview, Oppen glossed this poem as follows: "There is a feeling of something false in overprotection and over-luxury—my idea of categories of realness."[54] The sealed windows of the closed car are a barrier to vision, knowledge, and contact for both the observer and the limousine's disembodied occupant; the recurring image of glass in *Discrete Series* reaches its maximum opacity in this poem. The alienated and alienating character of this object is emphasized by its juxtaposition with the poem beginning "The mast" (reproduced on page 83), situated opposite from it in the Objectivist Press edition of the text. Whereas the sealed windows of the car deflect and thwart the perceiver's gaze, in "The mast" the eye encompasses the entire scene—it takes in the moving tip of the mast, the swelling sail, the warm wood of the deck, and finally even the "Rocks, sand, and unrimmed holes" that pass under the moving sailboat. For a skilled sailor such as Oppen, images of the sea (the sailboat becomes an organic component in this scene of cosmic harmony) always constitute privileged moments that present the "really real." The fluency of expression in "The mast" contrasts sharply with the abrupt rhythms of "Closed car," signaling the integration of the poem's referential and textual functions in the presentation of such an image.

THE LYRICAL EYE

Human vision provides the means by which we may occasionally grasp "the benevolence of the real,"[55] expressed in moments of what Oppen sometimes called "awe." Such a moment comprises the erotic center of *Discrete Series:*

She lies, hip high,
On a flat bed
While the after-
Sun passes.

Plant, I breathe——
                O Clearly,
Eyes legs arms hands fingers,
Simple legs in silk.
    (*NCP,* 20)

This lyric represents one of only three appearances of the first-person pronoun in *Discrete Series,* notably the only instance when the "I" is not interrogated. In this moment of clarity ("O Clearly") the mood is hushed and reverent. This image of a woman reclining in a classic odalisque posture seems to occur both in- and outside at once. The perceiving eye, like a breathing camera, plants itself in both space and time, attending to each particular in its turn, beginning with the woman's eyes. Oppen's words assert the simple but astonishing fact that this woman—Mary—is really there, not just as an object but as a perceiving subject as well. In the serial poem "Route" (*Of Being Numerous* [1968]), Oppen states his conviction that "Clarity, clarity, surely clarity is the most beautiful / thing in the world" (*NCP,* 193). Oppen's credo, stated in that poem, can be read as a declaration of documentary intent: "A limited, limiting clarity / I have not and never did have any motive of poetry/But to achieve clarity" (*NCP,* 193). Oppen valued those limits, such as the focal point of the lens, that set off and frame a space, enabling us to concentrate our attentions on the things inside, as in "Party on Shipboard" in *Discrete Series* where the eye sees the "Wave in the round of the port-hole / Springs, passing,——arm waved, / Shrieks, unbalanced by the motion—— / Like the sea incapable of contact / Save in incidents" (*NCP,* 15).

I'd like to contrast this erotic lyric with another in the series in which Oppen uses metaphor to show how machines can shape perception:

Near your eyes—
Love at the pelvis
Reaches the generic, gratuitous
                (Your eyes like snail-tracks)

Parallel emotions,
We slide in separate hard grooves
Bowstrings to bent loins,
                Self moving
Moon, mid-air.
                (*NCP,* 26)

Here Oppen describes the relationship between the two lovers in mechanical terms (which might bring to mind Marcel Duchamp's "Large Glass," or maybe some of the machine paintings of Francis Picabia) to objectify the condition of inevitable separateness that two individuals experience, no matter how physically enmeshed they may be. (The references to bowstrings and the moon in this poem make me think of the goddess Diana and her desire to be "Self moving" and chaste, although I am fairly certain Oppen did not intend to reference mythology here.) Marjorie Perloff takes a stab at trying to interpret these lines and momentarily risks sounding ludicrous. However, I think Perloff is correct in her assessment that "Making love, as the poem implies, is at once an act of conjunction and separation."[56] I don't believe the mechanical image is necessarily intended to convey a negative charge in this context, however. Even good sex can be a mechanical act. The series as a whole contains, as we have seen, many instances where machines seem to extend or blur into human functions and have positive or at least ambiguous connotations.

The evolutionary process that *Discrete Series* traces emerges in yet another "Mary poem":

No interval of manner
Your body in the sun.
You? A solid, this that the dress
                insisted,
Your face unaccented, your mouth a mouth?
                Practical knees:
It is you who truly
Excel the vegetable,
The fitting of grasses—more bare than

that.
Pointedly bent, your elbow on a car-edge
Incognito as summer
Among mechanics.
(*NCP,* 28)

Only George Oppen could write a love poem like this one. The image presents a kind of relaxed companionship between machine and human components: "Pointedly bent, your elbow on a car-edge." The poem explores the problem of the relation of the trace (in this case, the photograph of Mary that the poem describes) to the real Mary, which is also the problem of whether we can ever really know another ("Your body in the sun. / You?"). The Other is that elusive entity that somehow remains incognito despite the immediate evidence of the body filling clothes, solid enough to block sunlight and leave its precise geometries in the photographic film.

THE MISSING I

If the you, the Other, is mysteriously elusive as this poem suggests, the I is not. Oppen's insistence that "the self is no mystery" helps to explain why the first-person pronoun is practically absent from these poems; it occurs only three times in *Discrete Series,* only to be interrogated in one manner or another: "But if I (how goes / it?)." Like the photographer, the perceiving subject in these poems remains largely out of sight. Yet a distinct sensibility operates at the base of these perceptions, and the I/eye emerges obliquely in a number of ways. The second person appears with some frequency, gesturing to another (often Mary Oppen in George's ongoing conversation with her) and outward toward the reader, too, while implying a first person; the plural pronoun (which includes the "I" in a community) also occurs but nearly as tentatively as the first person. Beginning in the midst of a discussion ("you were / saying") and ending on the telephone ("Successive / Happenings / [the telephone]"), *Discrete Series* encloses in its dialogic parentheses a series of conversational fragments and builds a social world, a network of relations, from these materials.

OPPEN'S ETHICAL STANCE

By virtue of its serial, "open" form and its content (the local and particular; subjects not generally found in poetry, such as elevators and "The middle-aged man sliding / Levers in the steam-shovel cab"), Oppen's earliest work reflects an ethical stance similar to that which characterized documentary expression during the thirties. Central to this ethics is Oppen's conception of the dialectical relations between the part and the whole, the particular and the universal, and the individual and "the world, weather-swept, with which / one shares the century." The key word here is *shares*; in a discussion regarding "The knowledge not of sorrow," Oppen characterized the Marxism of *Discrete Series* as "the struggle against the loss of the commonplace."[57] For Oppen, this struggle manifested itself in language, in the poem's function as a common place. In his discussion of Oppen's poem "Vulcan" (1962), Harvey Kail notes that

> the test of truth (or at least of "sincerity") in a poem is its ability to establish for the poet and for the reader a tangible awareness of shared experiences among men and women that defines each of us as members of a human community.[58]

During the 1930s, documentary images served a similar function: to constitute a shared experience (a "common place") and to dispel alienation by linking the lives of the individuals pictured in the photographs with those who learned something about them by viewing them. Documentary aims to make another person's experience real to us. A good documentary photograph will enable a viewer to envision someone else's life (generally a more difficult life) and to imaginatively share in that person's experiences.

Alan Golding's contention that "The neutrality of tone and presentation of a documentary poetics make it a non-partisan poetics"[59] does not take into account that documentary expression in the thirties embodied a political stance that was decidedly leftist, populist, and pro-labor. Further, the "neutrality of tone and presentation" that Golding mistakes for non-partisanship was directly associated with documentary photography, which had distinct political affiliations.

The nature of these affiliations came under increasing scrutiny during the Depression. The Oppens' commitment to social concerns is demonstrated by the fact that in 1935 they joined the Communist Party and organized for the Workers Alliance, doing what is now called "outreach" with the unemployed in Brooklyn.

> . . .
> Among these streets where Petra beat
> A washpan out her window gathering
> A crowd like a rescue. Relief,

As they said it, The Relief.
(from "Return," *NCP,* 49)

In his book *Radical Visions and American Dreams,* Richard Pells describes the 1930s as a decade when people tended to regard private experiences in terms of public events and to think in terms of social solutions to personal problems. Pells believes this was especially true for the many writers who were in their thirties during the Depression. A young man like Oppen, who came of age with the twentieth century (he was born in 1908), certainly pondered the relationship between the individual and history. Marxism offered one way of understanding the nature of this relationship, poetry another.

SERIAL STRUCTURE

This land:
The hills, round under straw;
A house

With rigid trees

And flaunts
A family laundry,
And the glass of windows
(*NCP,* 16)

As Oppen once explained to Rachel Blau DuPlessis, a "discrete series" is a mathematical term for "a series in which each term is empirically justified rather than derived from the preceding term"[60]—that is, the next term cannot be predicted on the basis of any mathematical rule governing the series. In the same letter Oppen offers an example of such a series drawn from his immediate surroundings: "14, 28, 32, 42 . . . the names of the stations on the east side subway"[61] circa 1934; Oppen would later regret not adding this particular discrete series to his book's flyleaf. In *Meaning a Life,* Mary Oppen describes how she and George explored Manhattan and Brooklyn at the end of 1920s, riding the train and popping up at various subway stops to see what they might find aboveground.[62] Another example of a discrete series would be laundry strung along a clothesline, as in the poem reprinted above.

Applied to poetry, a discrete series is an "open" form since it displays a paratactic structure, where the elements do not "follow" from one another, and the reader does not require the information from any one section to understand the others. "Drawing," one of the last poems in *Discrete Series,* presents an image of such a form and how it unfolds: "Not by growth / But the / Paper, turned, contains / This entire volume" (*NCP,* 33). The serial poem qualifies as an open form since its generating principal cannot determine, by itself, a point of closure. According to Barbara Herrnstein Smith, the elements in a series "can be omitted, added, or exchanged without destroying the coherence or effect of the poem's thematic structure."[63] While we encounter, in our reading, the parts of Oppen's series in the particular order in which he has presented them, their potential for recombination acknowledges that meaning does not adhere in one particular arrangement.

Examining the history of this work, one discovers that the particular arrangement appearing in *New Collected Poems* (2002) is just the most recent of several provisional configurations it assumed along the way. In the Objectivist issue of *Poetry* (February 1931), under the title "1930'S [sic]" Oppen published two poems ("Thus / Hides" and "The knowledge not of sorrow," in that order) that would later become components of the 1934 edition of *Discrete Series* published by the Objectivist Press. Oppen subsequently repositioned "The knowledge not of sorrow" as the opening poem in the series, a placement that significantly alters its emphases. The poem beginning "White" was also published under the title "1930'S" in *An "Objectivists" Anthology* (1932). The January 1932 issue of *Poetry* included "Discrete Series I–IV" by "George A. Oppen." This sequence concludes with "The mast" (there entitled "Cat-Boat"), which appears in the final version of *Discrete Series* with a few revisions in punctuation and line breaks; poems I–III remained uncollected until the 2002 publication of *New Collected Poems.*

By structuring his poems as a discrete series, Oppen purposely avoided superimposing a larger, *a priori* structure of meaning on his materials. The discipline of poetic sincerity that informs these poems required that Oppen reject such a structure as falsifying. Instead, believing that meaning cannot be imposed upon the poem but must arise from the perceptions of the poet, he set about constructing a meaning built from Imagist, or empiricist, statements. Each image, constitutes a proof, a moment when one may grasp "the fact of the matter" in one's mind. One reads such a poem by moving from image to image, encountering the epistemological toeholds the poet has crafted in the bedrock of reality. Structuring a poem in this manner, Oppen moves with great caution and deliberateness from one word to another, like a climber driving a series of pitons into a rockface; each image, each statement, must be tested and deemed secure before he can confidently proceed to the next one: "Having a line a place to stand it is possible to take another step—"[64] Oppen wrote. Regarding the period of poetic silence that took place between *Discrete Series* and *The Materials,* he was fond of saying that "it took me twenty-five years to write the next poem," a remark that reveals the serial nature of Oppen's entire body of work.

OPPEN'S DOCUMENTARY METHOD

Once a linguistic object has been tested in this manner, it retains its integrity and may be used in the making of other poems, other written structures. Oppen's method of returning to his own words and moving them into new contexts embodies a unique documentary practice he initiated in *Discrete Series* and which he continued to employ, in both his poetry and correspondence, throughout his life. In his serial poem "Route" (1968), Oppen revisits some lines from *Discrete Series*:

> Reality, blind eye
> Which has taught us to stare—
>
> Your elbow on a car-edge
> Incognito as summer,
> I wrote. Not you but a girl
> At least
>
> (*NCP,* 193)

In addition to many passages from his own poems and correspondence, Oppen appropriated preexisting text from letters, prose, graffiti, song lyrics, and conversation, and recontextualized these documentary fragments, often repeatedly, within his own writing. Lines written by another sometimes assumed a talismanic significance in Oppen's life: He was convinced that Reznikoff's image of "a girder / Still itself among the rubbish" helped him retain his sanity through the carnage of World War Two. In *Discrete Series,* Oppen's use of Henry James's lines from "The Story in It," quoted snatches of conversation ("'O—' / 'Tomorrow?'—") and song lyrics ("'O city ladies'" from Ben Jonson), as well as preexisting images such as the Civil War photo, the female figures in a Jean-Honoré Fragonard painting ("Fragonard, / Your spiral women / By a fountain"), and a snapshot of Mary Oppen represent the earliest manifestations of this documentary practice in Oppen's work. *Discrete Series* itself was a text that Oppen consistently revisited throughout his life; its significance was due, in part, to its status as a document of the 1930s, an absolutely formative period for Oppen:

The Thirties. And
A spectre

In every street,
In all inexplicable crowds, what they did then
Is still their lives.
(*NCP,* 52)

These lines appear in "Blood from the Stone," the first poem Oppen wrote after his long silence. In the course of *Discrete Series,* Oppen initiated many of the themes he would go on to explore in poetry (" . . . I have thought, all my life, about those themes, have lived all my life on those emotional responses to 'the world'"[65]).

Oppen's appropriation and recontextualization of lines and images constitutes a documentary practice that purposefully exploits the tensions in his poetry between the contradictory objectives of linguistic transparence and textual opacity. Oppen's documentary poetic also discloses the dual nature of documentary itself: documentary as the presentation of truth, on the one hand, and documentary as a process of appropriation and recontextualization, on the other. In Oppen's poetry, documentary evidence in the form of a reappropriated phrase or image affirms and reaffirms its integrity as truth within the network of relations that is the medium of language.

A BACKWARD GLANCE

In 1936, James Agee declared that

> the camera can do what nothing else in the world can do: . . . perceive, record, and communicate, in full unaltered power, the peculiar kinds of poetic vitality which blaze in every real thing and which are in great degree . . . lost to every other kind of art.[66]

I detect a note of envy here. Working with Walker Evans to report on the conditions of tenant farmers in the South, Agee had plenty of opportunities to compare Evans's photography and his own prose as methods for documenting reality. Fiercely committed to the truth (reportedly he once hit a woman over the head with a chair because he believed she had faked an orgasm), Agee came to feel that language must ultimately fail in the attempt to capture reality, that there will always be a slippage between word and object, and that no final correspondence between the two is possible.

Clearly Oppen arrived at another conclusion: "I might at the top of my ability stand at a window / and say, look out; out there is the world" (*NCP,* 193). Objectivist poetics presupposes that existence precedes perception, and that language follows both. Through the resulting gap between perception and verbalization arises the possibility for an authentic encounter with the world, what the French philosopher Maurice Merleau-Ponty calls "the decisive moment of perception: the upsurge of a true and accurate world."[67] For Oppen, vision is the preeminent faculty because it affords us, on occasion, direct access to that world, and is thus one of the principal means by which we situate ourselves within it and in relation to others ("The eye *sees!* It floods in on us from here to Jersey tangled / in the grey bright air!" [*NCP,* 70]). The image that initiates *Discrete Series,* Maude Blessingbourne's act of looking through the window and out into the world is, simultaneously, an image of mediation—a pane of glass stands between Maude and what she perceives, and the window itself frames the scene that she observes. Still, it is Maude's desire that prompts the act of looking, and in desiring to know, she sees.

Discrete Series would remain Oppen's only published work until *The Materials* was issued in 1962. The appearance of this volume at the beginning of a poetic career that would only be publicly resumed nearly three decades later has had the effect of falsely isolating these poems from Oppen's later work, suggesting they might best be understood as a kind of modernist period piece. *Discrete Series* is, and necessarily so given the nature of its poetic, very much a document of its time and place. Still, these do not strike us as the poems of a young man so much as of one who has begun, with great care and deliberation, the exacting work of a life in poetry.

We had seen bare land
And the people bare on it
And men camp
In the city. The lights,
The pavement, this important device
Of a race. I wrote then,
Twenty three years old,
Remains till morning. Nobody knows who died
On the roads of that time, of the fact of roads.
I am a man of the Thirties

'No other taste shall change this'
("Memory at 'The Modern'" [*NCP,* 295])

Chapter Four

Machines for Seeing: William Carlos Williams's *Collected Poems 1921–1931*

> The photographic camera and what it could do were peculiarly well suited to a place where the immediate and the actual were under official neglect.
>
> —William Carlos Williams, in his essay "America and Alfred Stieglitz" (1934)

In many ways, 1934 was a banner year for Objectivist poetics. Despite the fact that it marked the trough of the American depression and money was hard to come by, in that year the Objectivist Press—a small press funded by a collective of poets committed to seeing their work in print—managed to issue three volumes that would become highly respected modernist texts. I have already discussed two of these: Charles Reznikoff's *Testimony* and George Oppen's *Discrete Series*, both published that year. Prior to these publications, in January of 1934, the Objectivist Press issued its first book: *Collected Poems 1921–1931* by William Carlos Williams. This 134-page volume, handsomely printed in an edition of 500 copies and priced at two dollars, brought together poems that would eventually be ranked with Williams's best in a collection that has been called "the most unjustly underrated volume of poems in all of Williams's work."[1]

Williams was fifty when his *Collected Poems* was published. Although he had placed individual poems in many of the little magazines that flared into life during that decade only to fizzle out after a few issues (*Blast, Blues, Contact*—which vowed to "cut a trail through the American jungle without the use of a European compass"—*Contempo, Pagany,* and *Symposium,* to name a few), Williams had yet to see his published verse assembled in a single book. Williams himself was convinced of the value of such a volume: In a

1933 letter to Pound he groused that he'd had no luck finding a publisher for "a volume of verse which I have been in the process of making for the last ten years, that is the best collection of verse in America today."[2] When the members of the Objectivist Press (Louis Zukofsky, George Oppen, and Charles Reznikoff, with Pound on the editorial board) agreed to put out the book, Williams was delighted. As he recalled in *I Wanted to Write a Poem,* "The suggestion to collect my poems was a lovely gesture from my own gang and I was deeply moved by it. Louis Zukofsky did most of the work of making the collection. Needless to say, it didn't sell at all."[3] Williams's memory was faulty: In fact, the edition of 500 copies nearly sold out, and in the United States alone the book was reviewed in the *New York Times Book Review, Poetry, New Republic,* the *Nation,* and the *New York Herald Tribune.* It earned mostly favorable notices, including praise from fellow poets Marianne Moore and Basil Bunting. In *Hound & Horn,* H. R. Hays called the *Collected Poems* "a lyric event of the highest importance" and advised "Let us hope the Pulitzer Prize Committee of 1934 makes no mistake."[4] (Alas, Robert Hillyer's *Collected Verse* was awarded that year's prize. Williams would not win the Pulitzer until 1963, for *Pictures from Brueghel and Other Poems.*) Williams's inability to recall his own success suggests his tendency to feel persistently neglected, but it also says something about those times: The no-nonsense thirties was, by and large, a tough time to be in the poetry business.

Collected Poems 1921–1931 is not strictly true to the chronology of its title, since it also includes a final section of poems written before 1921. Furthermore, the poems are not grouped in anything approaching chronological order. But a glance through the contents confirms Williams's belief in the worth of what is gathered here: "Young Sycamore," "It Is a Living Coral," "The Cod Head," "The Attic Which Is Desire," "This Is Just to Say," "The Botticellian Trees," along with poems from *Spring and All:* "The Red Wheelbarrow," "Rapid Transit," "To Elsie," and selections from *The Descent of Winter* including "A Morning Imagination of Russia." Williams's friend Wallace Stevens contributed the preface, aspects of which infuriated Williams, although not enough to persuade him to publish the book without it.

The fact that *Discrete Series, Testimony,* and *Collected Poems 1921–1931* were all issued by the Objectivist Press in the same year is certainly evidence that a poetic sympathy existed among these writers, that they believed in the kind of work they were doing, and wanted to tangibly support one another (often economically, since money was pooled to produce these books) in their various enterprises. The sincerity of their association and the commonality of their poetic goals at a particular historical moment are indisputable. Williams associated closely with the Objectivist poets, especially Zukofsky, with whom he had a long friendship and who served on many occasions as his editor. Williams's work appeared alongside poems by Zukofsky, Oppen, and Reznikoff in the "Objectivists" issue of *Poetry* (February 1931) as well as in the "Objectivists" anthologies that Zukofsky published in the following years. Reciprocally, Williams published work by Oppen, Reznikoff, and Zukofsky in the magazines he edited, such as *Contact.*

Discussions of Williams's poems frequently liken the visual movements of the perceiving subject to that of a "camera eye." As in the case of both Reznikoff and Oppen, metaphors and analogies drawn from photography and optics are ubiquitous in critical discussions of Williams's work. "Eyes have always stood first in a poet's equipment"[5] he wrote Zukofsky in 1928, and highest among his own capacities he rated "my sight. I like most my ability to be drunk with a sudden realization of value in things others never notice."[6] Reviewing the *Collected Poems 1921–1931* in the *New York Herald Tribune* (1 April 1934), Babette Deutsch emphasized Williams's association with the Imagists and concluded: "The reliance on the eye, the singling out of the brief moment, is a limitation upon his work."[7] In a characteristically ambivalent little piece entitled "Rubbings of Reality," Wallace Stevens wrote: "Williams is a writer to whom writing is the grinding of a glass, the polishing of a lens by means of which he hopes to be able to see clearly."[8] More recently, Bram Dijkstra describes some early poems from *Al Que Quiere!* (1917) as forming "essentially a suite of photographic images,"[9] and Williams's biographer Paul Mariani has referred to the "photographic realism" of the poems Williams wrote during his association with the Objectivist poets.[10]

THE POEM AS OBJECT

In the February 1931 issue of *Poetry* magazine, the "Objectivists" number that he had edited, Zukofsky used terms with optical/photographic and martial connotations to sketch out the parameters for a poetic theory:

> *An Objective: (Optics)—The lens bringing the rays from an object to a focus. (Military use)—That which is aimed at. (Use extended to poetry)—Desire for what is objectively perfect, inextricably the direction of historic and contemporary particulars.*[11]

Years later, Williams enlarged upon this theory in his *Autobiography* (1948):

> [T]he poem, like every other form of art, is an object, an object that in itself formally presents its case and its meaning by the very form it

> assumes. Therefore, being an object, it should be so treated and controlled—but not as in the past. For past objects have about them past necessities—like the sonnet—which have conditioned them and from which, as a form itself, they cannot be freed.
>
> The poem being an object (like a symphony or cubist painting) it must be the purpose of the poet to make of his words a new form: to invent, that is, an object consonant with his day.[12]

In the "Objectivists" issue of *Poetry*, Zukofsky cites Williams's work in *Spring and All* (1923) as satisfying the dual criteria of "sincerity" and "objectification" that help distinguish the poem as object. Williams's poem "The Botticellian Trees" (later included in *Collected Poems 1921–1931*) also appeared in the issue.

Zukofsky's statements in *Poetry* were preceded by "American Poetry from 1920–1930" (1930), an essay prominently featuring Williams, and Zukofsky's critical insights into his poetry. He points to Williams's "exclusion of sentimentalisms, similes, overweening autobiographies of the heart . . . of all but the full sight of the immediate."[13] Zukofsky first met Williams in the spring of 1928, at Pound's urging: "Do go down an' stir up ole Bill Willyums, 9 Ridge Rd. Rutherford (W. C. Williams M. D.) and tell him I told you. He is still the best human value on my murkn. visiting list."[14] Pound's introduction prompted a long and productive friendship, partially documented in the nearly 500 letters Williams addressed to Zukofsky over the years. Though Zukofsky was more than twenty years his junior, Williams was quick to place his work in Zukofsky's skillful editorial hands. The visual and optical terms Zukofsky often uses to characterize Williams's work ("the swift hold of art on things seen, in the sudden completeness of the word envisioning them," "a vision amid pressure," "his visioned impact against the environment," for instance) and Zukofsky's decision to frame a new poetic theory in photographic terms are expressions of an American culture preoccupied with new visual technologies and their ability to make a record of "the real."

Let us review the evidence, then: Criticism of Williams's work has tended to be oculocentric, taking the poet at his word when he privileges vision among his poetic faculties. For a time, Williams was profoundly influenced by Pound's Imagism, which called for presentation rather than re-presentation and a purified diction as spare and clean-edged as a black-and-white photograph. With poets such as Oppen, Reznikoff, and Carl Rakosi, with whom he associated during the thirties, Williams went on to articulate an Objectivist theory of the poem that adhered to many of the tenets of Imagism but reasserted the importance of form—a property Williams conceived of (as we will see) in largely visual/spatial terms. Williams's famous motto "No ideas but in things," a phrase that occurs in the first versions of *Paterson,* would seem to qualify Williams as a documentary poet, especially considering his use of documentary materials in *Paterson.* His desire "to find an image large enough to embody the whole knowable world"[15] certainly sounds like a job for a documentary poetic in the sense that I have employed the term.

Zukofsky locates a documentary impulse in Williams's poetry, which he describes as "the attractions of living recorded—the words a shining transcript."[16] I am interested in seeing how this impulse manifests itself in the verse Williams assembled in the *Collected Poems 1921–1931.* Reading Williams's poetry in relation to the documentary culture in which he and these poets was immersed during the 1930s will, I believe, shed some light on the following question: Does Williams's earlier verse qualify as a kind of documentary poetry? And did Williams's work embody the documentary paradox that I have identified, in which a fantasy of direct, unmediated contact with actuality is figured in terms of different forms of mechanical mediation, specifically the mechanisms of the camera?

THE POEM AS MACHINE

The previous chapters examine how Reznikoff and Oppen appropriated the technologies of the camera, a machine specifically designed to extend human perception. By enlarging the capacity of the human eye (and, by extension, that of the mind), the camera blurs the distinction between human subject and object, rendering them coextensive. Reznikoff and Oppen embodied this transformation in their writing, where they sought to blur prevailing distinctions between the subjectivity of art and the "objectivity" of the document. A decade after the publication of *Collected Poems 1921–1931,* it was Williams who welded poetry and technology together into a single memorable image. As he wrote in his introduction to *The Wedge* (1944):

> To make two bald statements: There's nothing sentimental about a machine, and: A poem is a small (or large) machine made of words. When I say there's nothing sentimental about a poem I mean that there can be no part, as in any other machine, that is redundant.[17]

The ideas Williams presents here came from a talk he gave at the New York Public Library in the fall of 1943. American industry was busy churning out parts and munitions for the war effort, a subject on Williams's mind when he spoke at the library that October evening; he was still thinking of war when he wrote the introduction to *The Wedge,* which begins: "The war is the first and only thing in the world today"(255). Williams's famous figure of the poem as machine is an expression of, as Cecelia Tichi has shown, the industrial "gear-and-girder" culture that radically changed the way we conceive of "reality" and its operations.[18] Related inspirations may include Stein's radical experiments with language ("Think of Gertrude Stein: to use words as objects out of which you manufacture a little mechanism you call a poem which has to deliver the goods"[19]) and Louis Zukofsky, who helped edit *The Wedge* and to whom the book is dedicated.[20] Williams's definition has a number of implications that Tichi explores, all of which are pertinent to this discussion: To understand the poem as a machine serves to highlight poetry's function as a device for transferring energy from poet to reader; as is the case in any well-designed and efficient machine, only the necessary parts are included—anything merely decorative or inessential to the mechanism's operation is redundant, or as Williams wrote, "sentimental"; and finally, by saying that a poem functions, literally, as a kind of mechanism, Williams implies that the word-objects comprising it function as components and that these components, like machine components, may be prefabricated. Perhaps in response to the darker manifestations of industrial mass production in the Soviet gulags, the Nazi death camps, and the American war industry, Williams was moved to show, by virtue of his training as a physician and a healer, that a poem modeled on a machine need not be coldly mechanical—after all, the warm and living human body could be understood as an engine as well.

OF WHEELBARROWS AND CHICKENS

Collected Poems 1921–1931 materialized at a moment in time when the U.S. documentary movement was gathering force and starting to manifest itself throughout American culture. Documentary photography (the term wouldn't gain currency until a few years later) was the most visible symptom of that movement, and images by photographers such as Margaret Bourke-White, Arthur Rothstein, Berenice Abbott, Dorothea Lange, and Walker Evans would soon fill the pages of the many photo magazines inaugurated during the 1930s. If, as James Agee claimed, the camera was the central instrument of the time, did this transformative technology leave its traces in Williams's poetry? And given his belief that vision was the poet's preeminent faculty, was the poem-machine that Williams conceived of specifically a mechanism for seeing, like a camera?

With these questions in mind, I'd like first to consider that old chestnut "The Red Wheelbarrow," perhaps the only Williams poem immediately recognizable to the average American college student. Originally published in *Spring and All* (1923), this poem reappears in Williams's *Collected Poems 1921–1931* with a spanking new title nearly twice as wide as the poem itself. Tichi calls it the quintessential Williams machine poem, although it can be argued that Williams had yet to formulate the concept of the poem-machine that he presents in *The Wedge*; "The Red Wheelbarrow" and many of the pieces in *Collected Poems* were written more than twenty years earlier. It is difficult to see this old poem with fresh eyes, but a new poem can also be hard to see. In his review of *An "Objectivists" Anthology* (1932), in which seventeen of his own pieces were included, Williams wrote:

> The difficulty in facing a "new" work, critically, is first to see then to say something about it that in its particularity will be new also, certainly something that will be at least of an equal freshness with the work itself. But most often we set in motion an antiquated machine whose enormous creaking and heavy and complicated motions frighten the birds, flatten the grass and fill the whole countryside with smoke.[21]

It's a comical image, but Williams makes an important point: Machines are designed to suit the needs of the time; literary and critical mechanisms are likewise provisional and unique to each occasion, and they do grow obsolete. Do we still need to be shown how a poem can be made of anything? If so, then "The Red Wheelbarrow" remains a functioning machine, capable of creating an experience in which the reader is invited to participate:

> so much depends
> upon
>
> a red wheel
> barrow
>
> glazed with rain
> water
>
> beside the white
> chickens
> (*CP*, 95)

Regarded as an object on the page, the poem clearly has a distinct visual form: Its four double-line clusters are of uniform length and feature regular line breaks. Each two-line stanza consists of four words, three on the first line and one on the second, all arranged flush left. The exclusion of capital letters and the absence of punctuation (which would have been strictly ornamental here, since the sense doesn't require any) also create a homogeneity of appearance. The poem is syntactically uniform, too: Its sixteen words form a complete sentence, despite the lack of an initial capital and terminal punctuation. In comparison to Oppen's methods in *Discrete Series* and elsewhere, the lines are not cut in a manner that both creates and/or calls attention to the ambiguity inherent in the syntax. Williams has broken two compound words (wheel/barrow, rain/water) in order to emphasize each particular in the scene; otherwise the line breaks appear to be determined by a prevailing visual pattern and Williams's intention to transform verbal phrases into spatial ones.

Visual uniformity is echoed by aural uniformity: The syllable count goes 6, 5, 5, 6. The stresses fall approximately three to a line, if you read them that way. The diction is simple, straightforward, and free of ornamentation but for that word "glazed," about which entire articles have been written,[22] and which edges the discourse into the realm of metaphor. It might be an interesting exercise to trace the progress of "glazed" as it recurs in Williams's work; I will simply say here that it is also the name of a certain kind of paper ("glazed paper") on which photographs are reproduced. The word calls attention to the poem as a verbal artifact, pulling us back to the surface before we can lose ourselves in the pleasant little agricultural scene the words have been conjuring up; "glazed" points to the shiny surface of the poem-machine, and, by extension, to the poet as the assembler of these parts.

To return to the original question about whether the poem, like a camera, is a machine for seeing: "The Red Wheelbarrow" presents a visual arrangement, but not in the manner of a photograph. An image may be described as gradually emerging, as the poem is read, in the same way that a photographic print slowly comes to resolution in the developing bath, but we get no true sense here of a glimpse of reality's flow fixed in the emulsion or the trace of something that actually occurred at a given place and time. The trouble is that phrase "so much depends upon"; we get hung up on it because its claim seems in excess of the facts (the innocuous wheelbarrow, the usual chickens) as they appear.

THE AMERICAN IDIOM

Until now I have been principally concerned with describing how this poem appears on the page, that is, its presence as a visual object. However, in *The*

Wedge Williams states that the movement of language in a poem will be "distinguished in each case by the character of the speech from which it arises."[23] Over the course of his life Williams wrote a great deal about his belief that poetry should be based on what he called "the American idiom," a logical extension of his motto (as John Dewey originally wrote) that "the local is the only universal, upon that all art builds." Hugh Kenner has pointed out that it is practically impossible to imagine anyone actually uttering the sentence comprising "The Red Wheelbarrow."[24] However, this exercise by no means invalidates the fundamental role of speech in this poem. As different commentators have remarked, the poem enacts the process by which the homely, ordinary objects of the world are transformed by art into something universal and timeless. In this apotheosis of sorts, speech has been transformed as well, into a spatial pattern born of the phrases intrinsic to the English language.

But we are also witnessing the transformation of a formerly useful machine (a wheelbarrow) into something decorative: an art object. The wheelbarrow, the chickens, do not strike the mind's eye as specific objects—real things in the real world circa 1923—but rather as particular forms entering, before our very eyes, the timeless realm of art. The addition of a descriptive title seems to support this; originally assigned number XXII in *Spring and All*, the poem presents the process of attention by which the indefinite article transforms into the definite: any old wheelbarrow becomes *the* wheelbarrow. These are a few of the things this poem may help the reader to see.

SENTIMENTALITY AND THE ANTI-POETIC

Submitted to Kenner's little test, "The Red Wheelbarrow" may sound risibly inauthentic; nonetheless, one of the features of this poem is its sincerity, a quality that is available to the eye. Laid bare on the page, in the simplicity of its language and the brevity and compactness of its form, the mechanism offers itself to the reader, free from "typographical tricks,"[25] a poem the eye drinks neat. We can see immediately how the language is assembled and how it moves. Similarly, the inner workings of a machine may be inspected with the naked eye.

As I have noted with respect to documentary expression during the 1930s, sincerity can easily lapse into sentimentality, one of the occupational hazards of a realist or documentary aesthetic. In his preface to *Collected Poems 1921–1931,* Stevens cautions the reader that "In order to understand Williams at all, it is necessary to say at once that he has a sentimental side. Except for that, this book would not exist and its character would not be what it is."[26] Stevens identifies sentimentality as part of a binary system fueling

Williams's poetry: "[T]he essential poetry is the result of the conjunction of the unreal and the real, the sentimental and the anti-poetic, the constant interaction of two opposites" (Preface, 3). By "anti-poetic" Stevens means the actual, the grubby objects of daily life (wheelbarrows, chickens), those things (as Williams said) that others never notice: "To a man with a sentimental side the anti-poetic is that truth, that reality to which all of us are forever fleeing" (2). The anti-poetic, as Stevens describes it here, has a distinct documentary flavor: "[N]ow, in the midst of a baffled generation, as one looks out of the window at Rutherford or Passaic, or as one walks the streets of New York, the anti-poetic acquires an extraordinary potency" (2).

Stevens's use of the term "anti-poetic" angered Williams, however. Many years later, in *I Wanted to Write a Poem* (1976), his irritation was still apparent: "I didn't agree with Stevens that it was a conscious means I was using. I have never been satisfied that the anti-poetic had any validity or even existed."[27] Williams's statements in *The Wedge* may amount to a belated defense against the charge of sentimentality that Stevens links with realism. In his description of the poem as a machine, Williams equates redundancy with sentimentality: "There's nothing sentimental about a machine. . . . When I say there's nothing sentimental about a poem, I mean that there can be no part, as in any other machine, that is redundant."[28] Verbal economy then, in addition to helping create a sharply focused effect analogous to photographic realism, is a hedge against sentimentality since it leaves no room for sentiment to find expression. In reference to the citizens of Paterson, New Jersey (that city where his medical rounds often took him), Williams once unwittingly demonstrated how easily he could slip into sentimentality even while he was inveigling against it:

> I can't say I love it here. I'm not interested in being sentimental! These folks—they'd smell that rot in a second. I'm interested in them because they are the people I've known all my life—and they're the kind of people who *made* this country, worked and worked to build it up. . . . They came here from everywhere, and made this place, right here, their somewhere.[29]

Williams stayed angry because Stevens had hit a nerve: Williams was a romantic poet, and his romanticism was entirely characteristic of his time.

PREFABRICATED COMPONENTS

To return, then, to Kenner's argument, if the diction in "The Red Wheelbarrow" doesn't sound especially idiomatic, like actual spoken language, there are other poems in *Collected Poems* containing passages that do. During his travels between home and his medical practice, Williams constantly jotted down bits of found speech, local expressions, and turns of phrase that caught his ear. Robert Coles equates Williams's use of the American idiom with Walker Evans's approach to the photographic image: "His version of Evans's 'documentary style' was a vernacular not showily summoned out of a craving for distinction, but earned in the daily and various rounds of his several working lives."[30] Williams incorporated these little idiomatic speech bits, like prefabricated components, into many of the pieces in *Collected Poems 1921–1931.*

In poems such as "Hemmed-in Males," with its soliloquy of commiseration ("Poor George / he's got a job now as janitor / in Lincoln School but the saloon / is gone forever"), "The Sea-Elephant" ("They / ought / to put it back where / it came from"), and "Death" ("the dog won't have to / sleep on his potatoes / any more to keep them / from freezing—") Williams incorporates idiomatic objects verbatim into his text or at least creates the impression of having done so, a practice comparable to what Reznikoff achieves with legal documents in *Testimony.* "Brilliant Sad Sun" uses the prefabricated components of signage in the same way:

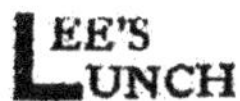

Spaghetti **Oysters**
a Specialty **Clams**

and raw Winter's done
to a turn—Restaurant: Spring!
Ah, Madam, what good are your thoughts

romantic but true
beside this gayety of the sun
and that huge appetite?

In "Rapid Transit," the rapid-fire presentation of a succession of advertisements enacts the mechanical accelerations of the subway train as it rattles along through the bowels of the city:

. . .
Outings in New York City
Ho for the open country!

Don't stay shut up in hot rooms
Go to one of the Great Parks

Pelham Bay for example
It's on Long Island Sound
with bathing, boating, golf, etc.

Acres and acres of green grass
wonderful shade-trees, rippling brooks

  Take the Pelham Bay Park Branch
  of the Lexington Ave. (East Side)
  Line and you are there in a few
  minutes

Interborough Rapid Transit Co.
(*CP*, 97)

Cecelia Tichi notes that the design of the poem is "formed largely of components manufactured, so to speak, in the word factories of the advertising agencies."[31] She points out that

> the experience of the poem is the experience of contemporary urban life, fast and disjunctive. Its components include advertising copy, slogans, maxims. All are prefabricated elsewhere and renewed by reformulation in poetic design.[32]

In "The Attic Which Is Desire," Williams also incorporates signage into the design of the poem, in this case typographically reproducing the vertical arrangement of a sign seen from a window:

. . .
from the street
by
  * * *
  * S *
  * O *
  * D *
  * A *
  * * *

ringed with running lights
(*CP*, 47)

Williams's incorporation of appropriated text into these verses anticipates his use of "documentary bits" (letters, historical prose, newspaper accounts, and other such materials) in *Paterson,* which Williams began work on as early as 1926.[33] Describing his working methods in *I Wanted to Write a Poem,* Williams reveals how he conceived of elements of *Paterson* in documentary terms:

> I used documentary prose to break up the poetry, to help shape the form of the poem. . . . The documentary notations were chosen for their live interest, their verisimilitude. Each Part of the poem was planned as a unit complete in itself, reporting the progress of the river.[34]

Especially worth noting here is Williams's remark that the "documentary notations" of *Paterson* were essential to the formal structure of that work. Williams's methods in poems such as "Brilliant Sad Sun" and "Rapid Transit" may be viewed as prototypes for the far more ambitious documentary project of *Paterson.* In *Collected Poems 1921–1931,* the "prefabricated bits" introduce documentary content into the verse, certainly, but they also represent part of Williams's effort to embody the new machine forms in language. In *Testimony,* Reznikoff's use of such "found" materials changes the relationship of the artist to the art: The poet becomes an editor and an assembler.

WILLIAMS AND WALKER EVANS

In the October 12, 1938, issue of the *New York Times,* Williams reviewed the published text of *American Photographs,* Walker Evans's solo show at the Museum of Modern Art (MOMA) in New York. Williams makes no overt reference to Evans's contribution to the documentary movement of the time, although he does remark that the eighty-seven photographs comprise "a record of what was in that place for Mr. Evans to see and what Mr. Evans saw there in that time."[35] In an earlier draft of this review, Williams also echoed Lincoln Kirstein's remarks, from the essay accompanying the photographs, about the relationship between Evans's work and the Civil War photographs of Mathew Brady:

> In Evans's pictures also we are seeing fields of battle after the withdrawal of the forces engaged. The jumbled wreckage, human and material, is not always so grim in the present case but for all the detachment of the approach the effect is often no less poignant.[36]

The capacity of an "objective" photograph to arouse our emotions impressed Oppen and Reznikoff, who aspired to this condition in their writing; Williams admired this aspect of Evans's work enough to mention it in his brief review. Kirstein was the editor of the influential literary journal *Hound & Horn,* where some of Brady's images had previously been reprinted (vol. VII, no. 1 [Oct./Dec. 1933]; see chapter 1, figures 1.5 and 1.6) and where Williams surely saw them. Williams recognized that Evans's images could provide the viewer with a visual education, and in discussing Evans's work he illuminates his own concerns and methods:

> I'm glad that Evans has promenaded his eyes about America rather than France in this case. We go about blind and deaf. We fight off convictions that we should welcome as water in the desert, could we possibly get ourselves into the right mind. The artist must save us.[37]

Throughout the piece, Williams sounds the notes of his familiar theme: how, through art, the local becomes the universal.

Williams knew Evans personally. As Robert Coles writes in *Doing Documentary Work,*

> Williams was among Evans's admirers; he followed his work closely, wrote about it. . . . Like Evans, Williams tried to come to grips with that word *documentary,* and made no bones about his belief that location and time mattered enormously: where one chose to stay and for how long, but also . . . "the language—and how it is used," by which he more broadly meant the relation of the watcher to the watched, of the one listening to those who fill his ears with words.[38]

In Williams's novel *A Voyage to Pagany* (1928), the protagonist, Dev Evans (a stand-in for Williams himself), sees the world with photographic precision.

WILLIAMS AND THE INFLUENCE OF STIEGLITZ

Walker Evans and Alfred Stieglitz each represent a different approach to photography and its significance in the modernist period, and each would prove to be a crucial figure in American cultural history. Any exploration of the role of photography in Williams's work must take into account Stieglitz's influence. Bram Dijkstra, Dickran Tashjian, and others have looked closely at Williams's associations with Stieglitz and the artists in his circle. Dijkstra goes so far as to credit these relationships with inspiring Williams's transformation from a derivative poet capable of not much more than bad Keats imitations to a strikingly original writer.[39] Many of the painters who influenced Williams, such as Charles Sheeler, Charles Demuth, and Juan Gris, were themselves influenced by photography.

The November 1922 issue of *Broom* magazine included an essay by the photographer Paul Strand entitled "Photography and the New God." Here Strand delineates the principles of Precisionism, the American movement (1917–1931) that celebrated the aesthetics of the machine and imagined the United States as an industrial Arcadia. Strand identifies Stieglitz as the artist who achieved the fullest expression of the camera's potential to create art, not in slavish imitation of painting but on its own terms. Stieglitz's magazine *Camera Work* (circa 1909) was printed on very high-quality paper, resulting in reproductions of images that were often indistinguishable from original prints, making the point in a very tangible and immediate way that a photograph could be a work of art.

The qualities Strand identifies with Stieglitz's mature work are characteristic of "straight photography," a style Strand was also associated with: an appearance of "objectivity" achieved in clear and sharply delineated images, features related to machine function and the aesthetics of Precisionism, as opposed to techniques of soft-focus and darkroom "tricks" for manipulating the image. It is significant that Stieglitz was, as Strand notes, "an American in America," echoing Stieglitz's own disapproval of expatriated Americans who believed that culture could only be found overseas, principally in Paris. According to Strand, the full potential of this new art could only be achieved in the "new world."[40]

In 1915, Marius de Zayas, a member of Stieglitz's circle, wrote: "Stieglitz, in America, through photography, has shown us, as far as it is possible, the objectivity of the outer world."[41] Covering the March 1921 retrospective of Stieglitz's work at the Anderson Galleries in New York, the artist Marsden Hartley wrote approvingly that: "[T]here is no mystery whatever in these productions, for they are as clear and I shall even go so far as to say objective as the daylight which produced them, and . . . they are as impersonal as it is possible for an artist to be."[42] In accounts such as these, the vocabulary of artistic appreciation seems nearly indistinguishable from that of scientific discourse; clearly, the function of the artist had undergone a radical change in the aftermath of the First World War: "[A]s far as art is concerned, the end of the world has been seen."[43] As Hartley summed it up, "Art these days is a matter of scientific comprehension of reality, not a trick of the hand or the old-fashioned manipulation of a brush or a tool. I am interested in presentation pure and simple."[44] These writers championed a view of art that aimed at a transcription of reality, in which fidelity to the object was of paramount concern, and where the artist's job was to see clearly and to present as straightforwardly as possible. As Strand put it, "the ideal artist would be selfless as a lens." This sounds like a precept that Charles Reznikoff, in particular, would have approved of, which is a point I will return to below.

A concept worth mentioning in this context is Stieglitz's notion of the *equivalent.* The term furnished the title for his famous series of cloud photographs, but Stieglitz also insisted that "in reality all my photographs are *Equivalents.*"[45] The concept of the equivalent is a version in the visual arts of T. S. Eliot's "objective correlative," an artistic formula designed to provoke a given emotion in the reader. Peter Schmidt equates the two when he writes that for the Precisionists, "each picture was primarily a portrait of emotion itself, an objective correlative, or equivalent."[46]

ANTI-ART

Walker Evans's attitude toward Stieglitz and his work was primarily negative. Stieglitz had originally shown no interest in Evans's early work, which may have given him a chip on his shoulder about the older artist. At any rate, Evans criticized Stieglitz for aestheticizing the photographic image, and he formulated his own "documentary style" partly in reaction to what Stieglitz stood for:

> He was undoubtedly the most insistently "artistic" practitioner of all time; with the adverse effect that it was he who forced "art" into quotation marks and into unwonted earnestness. On the other hand, Stieglitz's overstated, self-conscious aestheticism engendered a healthy reaction. We got a school of anti-art photography out of his protestations.[47]

(True perhaps, but whose "anti-art" photography earned him a solo show at the Museum of Modern Art?)

A powerful and charismatic figure, Stieglitz invariably inspired strong reactions among those who knew him. The ambivalence of Williams's own response to Stieglitz is evident in an essay he submitted for a volume of memorial tributes after the artist's death, which was subsequently rejected by its editor Dorothy Norman. "What of Alfred Stieglitz?" (1946), an intentionally iconoclastic essay marred by some false statements and anti-Semitism, is "a vivid testimony to the importance of Williams's indebtedness to Stieglitz."[48] The question of influence is especially pertinent with respect to Williams, Dijkstra argues. "Highly impulsive by nature, and often uncertain of his own opinions, [Williams] frequently depended on the judgment of others for direction in the focus of his ideas."[49] If this is true, it helps explain Williams's reluctance to frankly credit influences such as Louis Zukofsky ("the hidden unsung editor of all of Williams's substantial prose and poetry," according to Neil Baldwin,[50]) for fear of appearing derivative and unoriginal. Such fears, however, apparently did not dissuade Williams from the practice of basing his poems on preexisting works of art.

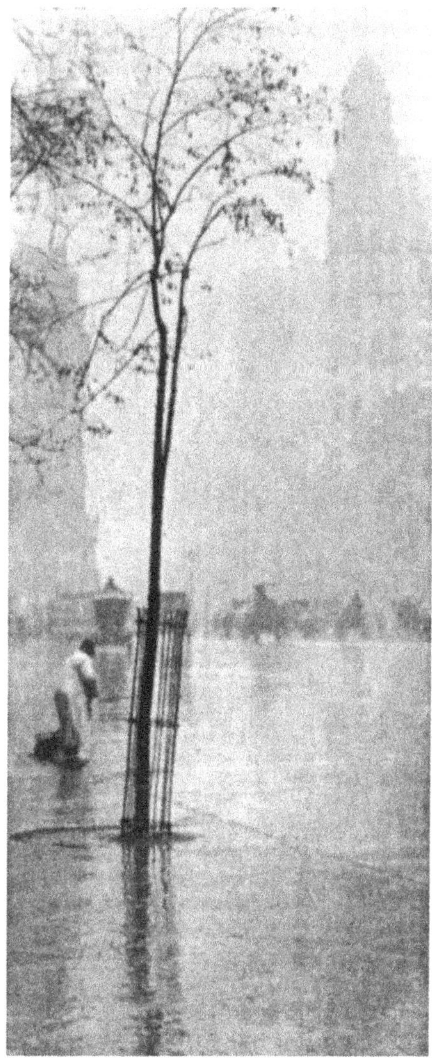

Fig. 4.1 Alfred Stieglitz. Street view in New York City (1902)
Library of Congress, Prints and Photographs Division, LC-USZ62-55089

POEMS FROM PAINTINGS

In *A Recognizable Image,* Dijkstra describes Williams's practice of translating paintings into poetry. In *Collected Poems 1921–1931,* for instance, the poem from *Spring and All* entitled "A Pot of Primroses" is "a literal transmutation" of Charles Demuth's watercolor *Tuberoses* (1922).[51] Dijkstra also argues that the poem "Young Sycamore" is a rendering of Stieglitz's photograph *Street view in New York City*, sometimes reproduced with the title *Spring Showers* (1902):

I must tell you
this young tree
whose round and firm trunk
between the wet

pavement and the gutter
(where water
is trickling) rises
bodily

into the air with
one undulant
thrust half its height—
and then

dividing and waning
sending out
young branches on
all sides—

hung with cocoons
it thins
till nothing is left of it
but two

eccentric knotted
twigs
bending forward
hornlike at the top
(*CP*, 10)

Dijkstra writes that "Williams's description of the tree . . . makes it correspond so minutely to the facts of Stieglitz's photograph that the possibility of coincidence seems highly unlikely."[52] I don't buy Dijkstra's argument here, for several reasons. I can't agree that the particulars of the poem correspond so closely to Stieglitz's image, and each work conveys an entirely different mood: That scrawny tree struggling crookedly out of its cage is no match for the erotic dynamism of Williams's sycamore. Williams always knew that nature is a lot sexier than a wheel rim, even when you drape Georgia O'Keeffe's hands over it. Comparing a poem such as "Young Sycamore" or "Rain" in this volume with the poems that take their forms from machines, one senses that Williams was always more at home working with, and within, organic forms as opposed to mechanical ones.

APPROACHES TO THE OBJECT

Precisionism shares certain similarities with Pound's Imagism and the poetics of Objectivism: An emphasis upon artistic sincerity (i.e., no tricks), the primacy of the object and the suppression of the subject, the absence of commentary, a preference for clean lines (whether visual or verbal), and the emphasis on presentation rather than representation are all qualities that recur, as we have seen, in discussions of the work of Stieglitz, Reznikoff, and Oppen. There are, however, important distinctions between Stieglitz's position and the stance taken by the Objectivist poets, especially with regard to the object, the thing itself. Stieglitz purposefully removed the object from its context and abstracted it, thus enabling it to become universal and transcendent. He accomplished this by focusing closely on his subject and eliminating its surroundings. Objects, such as that famous wheel rim, were not photographed in use. Oppen, on the other hand, wanted to attend to the object in context and to consider it in terms of its relationships. Throughout *Discrete Series* one finds objects and machines functioning as extensions of the human user (and vice versa), epitomized in the photographic image of Mary Oppen's "Pointedly bent" elbow on the ledge of the car window, "Incognito as summer / Among mechanics" (*NCP,* 28).

WILLIAMS AND OPPEN

In the preface to Oppen's *Discrete Series,* Ezra Pound makes a point of defending Oppen against the charge that his poems are like those of Williams. Pound's defense apparently had the opposite of its desired effect and instead encouraged readers to see likenesses between the two poets where few, in fact, exist. As Marjorie Perloff notes, "although his poems may look on the page like Williams's lyrics . . . Oppen's language, his syntax, and especially his prosody are really quite different."[53] Perloff examines prosodic differences in the work of these poets in her comparison of Williams's "Nantucket" from *Collected Poems* and Oppen's "She lies, hip high" from *Discrete Series,* both dating from 1934. Rather than reiterate Perloff's arguments, I'd like to extend some of her findings to each poet's treatment of the skyscraper, an architectural form that, perhaps more than any other, defined modernist aesthetics during the 1930s. Here is one of Williams's poems on the subject:

DOWN-TOWN

is a condition—
of bedrooms whose electricity

is brackish or made into
T beams—They dangle them

on wire cables to the tops
of Woolworth buildings

five and ten cents worth—
There they have bolted them

into place at masculine risk—
Or a boy with a rose under

the lintel of his cap
standing to have his picture

taken on the butt of a girder
with the city a mile down—

captured, lonely atop
iron girder wears rosepetal

smile—a thought of Indians
on chestnut branches

to end "walking on the air"
(*CP,* 26)

Here is Oppen's, from *Discrete Series,* published the same year:

White. From the
Under arm of T

The red globe.

Up
Down. Round
Shiny fixed
Alternatives

From the quiet

Stone floor . . .
(*NCP,* 6)

Looking at these examples, we don't need Pound to tell us how to differentiate between Williams's and Oppen's work—despite what Perloff says, the appearance of the poems on the page does that quite successfully. The

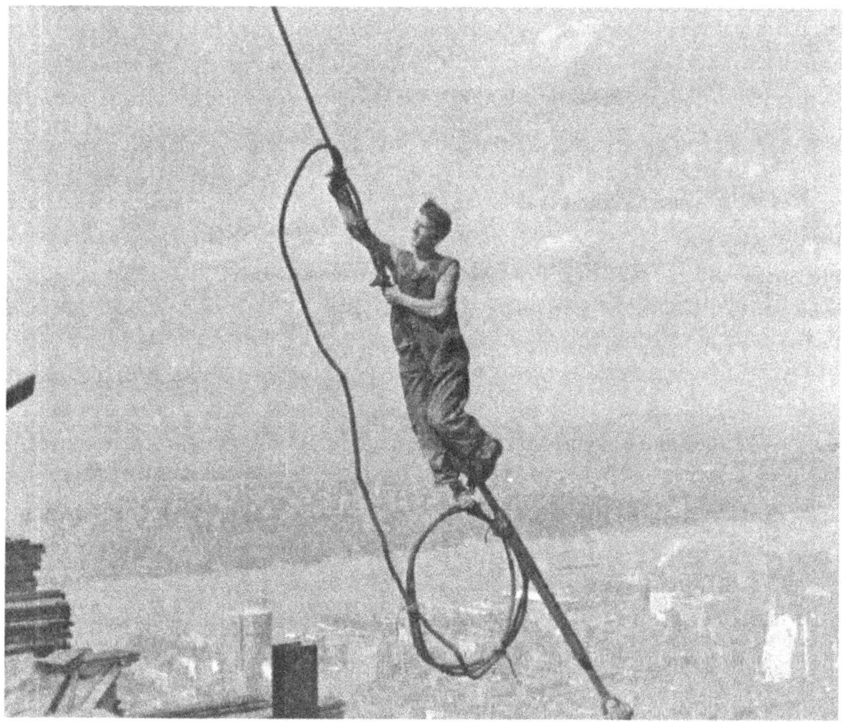

Fig. 4.2 Lewis Hine. Icarus high up on Empire State (1931)
Photography Collection, Miriam and Ira D. Wallach Division of Art, Prints and Photographs, The New York Public Library, Astor, Lenox and Tilden Foundations. Used with permission.

architectural aesthetics of the period made a virtue of clean lines, embodied in glass and metal forms that incorporated the steel beams of their support structures into their finished designs. When the George Washington Bridge in New York City was being built during the 1930s, the chief engineer wanted to omit the masonry facing on the towers so that the steel supports of the bridge would show.[54] The Empire State and the Chrysler Building were also completed by the early thirties; for years people had watched these structures in the process of being erected. If a poem is a machine made of words, then its components should be similarly subject to visual inspection, enabling the reader to figure out how its various parts fit together. One of these components—measurable and therefore objective—is its metrical structure. Other elements that contribute to the visual experience of a poem include the arrangement of type on the page, the use of white space, and typographical elements. Oppen's and Williams's verses, as Perloff and Kenner point out, feature effects intended solely for the eye, resonances and meanings that are lost when one simply hears the poem read aloud and does not see it on the page—for instance, the graphic design of the soda sign in Williams's "The Attic Which Is Desire" or the numerous syntactical ambiguities introduced by the line breaks throughout *Discrete Series.*

Both of the skyscraper poems reproduced above express the aesthetics embodied in that architectural form: Lines are broken and arranged to echo the narrow rectangular shape of a high-rise building, and decoration (that is, figurative language) has been avoided in favor of verbal economy. However, Oppen takes this to its extreme, reducing the language to its barest components, its most essential features and functions: *White. Red. Up. Down. Round. Shiny.* (See also my discussion of this poem in chapter 3.) Each word is weighed and tested, closely scrutinized to determine its integrity. Oppen shows us how a syntax might be built, from the ground up, that could support the weight of meaning pressing down upon it from above. The "quiet / Stone floor" that the mechanism of "White" rests upon is the "hard mineral fact" of the world.

In comparison, Williams could not resist the temptation to bring something horticultural into the poem: He's got to have that rose, those chestnut branches. "Down-Town" may well be a "translation" of a photograph—one thinks immediately of Lewis Hine's portraits of industrial laborers entitled *Men at Work* (1932) and his images of construction workers on the Empire State Building (see figure 4.2), and the mood is certainly similar. In contrast to Hine's earlier work for the Child Labor Committee, which exposed the practice of hiring underage workers and ultimately helped change labor laws (see chapter 2, "Documentary Matters," in which I compare Hine's work to that of Charles Reznikoff), Hine's heroic portraits of individual workers constitute a paean to human labor. Like Hine, Williams admires the romance of physical labor, the strength and poise of these structures and those who erect them ("they have bolted them / into place at masculine risk"), whether welder or poet.

To return to Pound's scolding preface to *Discrete Series,* it is perhaps worth comparing Oppen's "White" with an additional poem by Williams, featuring another significant component of the urban landscape, the tenement building.

TO

a child (a boy) bouncing
a ball (a blue ball)—

He bounces it (a toy racket
in his hand) and runs

and catches it (with his
left hand) six floors

straight down—
which is the old back yard
(*CP,* 15)

Looking at these two poems, one begins to see why Pound felt it necessary to declare, "I see the difference between the writing of Mr. Oppen and Dr. Williams, I do not expect any great horde of readers to notice it . . . they will coagulate their rather gelatinous attention on the likeness."[55]

In the *Collected Poems,* at least, Williams seems to have no quarrel with the medium of language itself, as long as it is the right language: the American vernacular. Unlike Oppen, Williams doesn't appear wary of the very components of the sentence as the supporting structure upon which perception and knowledge are built. While he pares down a sentence to its essentials and eliminates redundancies, Williams trusts, I believe, that the fundamental sentence structure—simple, declarative, communicative—the basic syntax itself is relatively pure and doesn't need to be disassembled. In this respect Williams shares Hemingway's belief in the possibility of the "One True Sentence" as the cornerstone of verbal construction. If a poem is a kind of machine, then Williams seems more or less convinced of the integrity of its component parts. Oppen's poetics, on the other hand, manifests no such assurance.

THE DOCUMENTARY PROJECTS OF WILLIAMS AND REZNIKOFF

In 1948, William Carlos Williams wrote a letter to Charles Reznikoff regarding his book *By the Waters of Manhattan: An Annual* (1929):

> A confession and an acknowledgement! In all the years that I have owned a book of yours, nineteen years! a book you gave me in 1929, I never so much as opened it—except to look at it cursorily. And now, during an illness, I have read it and I am thrilled with it. . . . [56]

This epistolary episode is emblematic of the interactions of these poets: Williams had occasions to admire Reznikoff's work; he published two installments of "My Country 'Tis of Thee" (the initial version of *Testimony*) in *Contact* (vol. 1, nos. 1 and 2) and got his buddy Kenneth Burke to write an introduction for *Testimony* when it was published by the Objectivist Press two years later. Otherwise, they were temperamentally very different creatures and did not spend much time in each other's company. Reznikoff said, "I had very little to do with Williams. . . ."[57]

Nonetheless, they had some common interests. Closer in age than the other poets associated with Objectivism (Williams was born in 1883, Reznikoff in 1894), both wrote immigrant histories (Williams's Sketcher trilogy, based on the life of his wife's family, and Reznikoff's *Early History of a Sewing Machine Operator*). More important, each was engaged in a long historical/poetic project that incorporated prodigious amounts of documentary materials in innovative ways. Each recognized, as well, that the problem of how to give form and meaning to these materials was essentially the central problem of modern life that the artist must address.

Describing his working methods in *Testimony,* Reznikoff noted how the legal case files from which he drew his materials were available to anyone, a wealth of factual material in the public domain. Reznikoff selected from hundreds of documents, which he then edited and arranged; however, much of the testimony was left in its original form. Reznikoff's methods provoked criticism that *Testimony* was comprised of mere transcriptions, raising questions about the artist's role in relation to his or her materials. Marcel Duchamp's readymades had prompted similar questions that were still being discussed more than a half century later, for instance, in the debate about music sampling.

Reznikoff, with his law degree, respected the precision of legal discourse and the way words were used for their "daylight meaning / and not as prisms / playing with the rainbows of connotation."[58] In a manner analogous to the way a lawyer assembles a case from the facts, doctors also assemble case histories, essentially narratives that impose form upon an assortment of facts that lead, ultimately, to a diagnosis and a course of treatment. Dr. Williams looked and listened to the people he interacted with in his daily rounds with an eye toward collecting details that caught his interest. Williams's working papers included a folder labeled "Detail & Parody for the Poem Paterson" full of materials he assembled in the late 1930s including poems, observed details, and bits of overheard conversation.[59] In *I Wanted to Write a Poem,* Williams recalls the research that went into his preparations for *Paterson:* "I read everything I could gather, finding fascinating documentary evidence in a volume published by the Historical Society of Paterson. Here were all the facts I could ask for, details exploited by no one."[60] Williams and Reznikoff both saw the potential of the public record as a source for poetry; they also recognized that its value, the facts this record "contained," were actually constituted in the language of the documents themselves. Williams said,

> I used documentary prose to break up the poetry, to help shape the form of the poem. Facts about the Indians, about colonial history, celebrated figures of the time appear in very much the same form as they appeared in the documents collected by the Paterson Historical Society. . . .[61]

What distinguishes Williams's and Reznikoff's work with documentary sources in *Paterson* and *Testimony,* respectively, is how they leave selected documentary texts largely intact and allow the materials themselves to suggest new poetic forms. Many commentators point to Williams's use of documentary materials as evidence of the impact of the Cubist painters on his work.[62] However, as Michael Davidson argues with reference to Reznikoff's *Testimony,* Williams's documentary assemblages in *Paterson* shift emphasis from "the materiality of aesthetic language to the materiality of social speech."[63] Within the poem itself and in his prose and criticism, Williams reiterated the importance of "the language, the language" (*Paterson,* 11), that is, speech as a common place within which our experiences of the world are constituted.

In the *Collected Poems 1921–1932,* the incorporation of quoted dialogue, advertising text, song lyrics, directional signage, menus, the captions under paintings (in "It Is a Living Coral"), and other "documentary bits" are all part of Williams's effort to objectify this "common place," to create the texture of the material world of social speech that we inhabit and to give it significant form in poetry. In *Collected Poems* we see him testing methods he will subsequently adapt to shape the form of *Paterson.*

REALITY AND IMAGINATION

Williams's insistence that "the local is the only universal" was a recurrent feature of his aesthetic thinking, a version of the contradiction central to documentary expression that I have explored in the work of Charles Reznikoff (see chapter 2, "Documentary Matters") and George Oppen (see chapter 3, "The Lyrical Apertures of George Oppen's *Discrete Series*"): the conviction that the so-called "objective" presentation of actuality must be grounded in the particular and the subjective. According to Williams, the true artist is a seer, and what he (the masculine pronoun is intentional) sees is Truth (the initial capital is also intentional) embodied in the objects he perceives with his senses. Dijkstra confirms that Williams

> equated the artist's attempts to record his perception of that objective reality with objectivity, the revelation of the universal in the particular. . . . [H]e did not at all contemplate the possibility that what he considered the "good" artist's "unaltered" perception of objective reality simply represented another manipulated mode of the conceptualization of that reality.[64]

Williams, like Reznikoff and Oppen, had a blind spot common to many people living at that particular time in history: They believed in the objective truth of sight, that our visual perception can and does, on occasion, afford us direct and unmediated access to reality itself.

However, where Williams believed in Truth, the Objectivist poets believed in truths, moments when, as Oppen wrote, "one cannot / Not see" (*New Collected Poems,* 185). As I have argued, this belief in human vision as an unmediated source of knowledge about the world was fundamental to the entire American documentary movement and especially to the camera work of the time as practiced by the Farm Security Administration photographers, under the guidance of FSA director Roy Stryker. Documentary photography in the 1930s relied on the assumption that vision is a form of epistemology: to see is to know.

In the opening prose passage of *Spring and All* (1923) Williams states, "There is a constant barrier between the reader and his consciousness of immediate contact with the world."[65] Most of the art of the past and certainly all of the writing, Williams claims, has been devoted to shoring up this barrier and mediating between the individual and that person's consciousness of the world. According to Williams, the imagination can pierce this interfering membrane and put the reader in direct contact with actuality. "To refine, to clarify, to intensify that eternal moment in which we alone live there is but a single force—the imagination."[66] Imagination, for Williams, meant a fusion of what Louis Zukofsky called the "clear physical eye" and the visualizing powers of the mind, the only means by which we may come to regard ourselves as coextensive with the universe rather than alienated from it. In his 1855 Preface to *Leaves of Grass,* Walt Whitman offered his own version of documentary sincerity when he wrote: "I will not have in my writing any elegance or effect or originality to hang in the way between me and the rest like curtains. I will have nothing hang in the way, not the richest curtains. What I tell I tell for precisely what it is."[67] Whitman is a strong presence here, as Williams concludes this passage of *Spring and All* by achieving imaginative contact with the reader: "We are one. Whenever I say, 'I' I mean also, 'you.' And so, together, as one, we shall begin."[68] Williams's desire for "contact" (he edited a quarterly magazine by that title) demanded poetic forms that present the unmediated object, the so-called "thing in itself." Louis Zukofsky, speaking for the Objectivists, proposed a theory of the poem that answered this demand for "writing which is an object or affects the mind as such."[69]

Over the course of *Paterson*'s evolution, Williams departed from his original plan to allow the materials of social speech to shape the poem's form. Later drafts reveal, for instance, that Williams drastically reduced the number of "contemporary particulars" he had originally included showing the life of the working classes in *Paterson.* When Book One was finally published in 1946, Williams had introduced the devices of metaphor and simile and the larger structures of myth in order to marshal his accumulated materials. No longer convinced that a poem—especially a long poem—could be constructed from the "bare facts" alone, Williams eventually resorted to the imaginative constructions that he understood as essentially organic, issuing from the body itself.

When he assembled the *Collected Poems 1921–1931,* Williams conceived of the poem not as a machine for seeing but more precisely as a machine for teaching the reader how to see. As he would remark a few years later in his review of Walker Evans's *American Photographs* (1938), "First we have to see, be taught to see. We have to be taught to see *here,* because here is everywhere, related to everywhere else."[70] In poem after poem Williams shows us exactly how it's done:

As the cat
climbed over
the top of

the jamcloset
first the right
forefoot

carefully
then the hind
stepped down

into the pit of
the empty
flowerpot
(*CP,* 35)

Notes

NOTES TO THE PREFACE

1. George Oppen quoted in *Contemporary Literature* 10 (Spring 1969), 161.

NOTES TO THE INTRODUCTION

1. "The Thirties," in *The Development of an American Culture,* 227.
2. *They Must Be Represented,* ix.
3. *Proletarian Literature in the United States,* 19.
4. Stott, 36.
5. "Poetry in America: Objectivism," trans. Richard Lebovitz, from "Poésie Objectiviste" (*Les Lettres Nouvelles,* 1967), *Ironwood* 6 (1975), 51.
6. *Selected Letters of George Oppen,* ix.
7. *Poetry* XXXVII, no. 5 (February 1931), 268.
8. "The Objectivist Tradition," 16.
9. *Carl Rakosi: Man and Poet,* 378.

NOTES TO CHAPTER ONE

1. Dembo interview in *Contemporary Literature* (Spring 1969), 203.
2. *Poetry* XXXVII, no. 5 (February 1931), 269.
3. *Poetry* I, no. 6 (March 1913).
4. "A Retrospect," 46.
5. "A Retrospect," 45.
6. *The Autobiography of William Carlos Williams,* 265.
7. *Poetry* XXXVII, no. 5 (February 1931), 274.
8. Kenner, *A Homemade World: The American Modernist Writers,* 167.

9. Interview with L. S. Dembo in *Contemporary Literature* (Spring 1969), 161, referred to hereafter as Dembo interview.
10. Dembo interview, 160.
11. *Selected Letters of George Oppen,* 82.
12. Altieri, 15.
13. Rabinowitz, 102.
14. Tichi, *Shifting Gears,* 229.
15. Curtis, *Mind's Eye, Mind's Truth,* vii.
16. "Epic, 'Action-Poem,' Cartoon," *Charles Reznikoff: Man and Poet,* 311.
17. "Politics and Style in Oppen's *Discrete Series,*" *Ironwood* 26, vol. 13, no. 2 (Fall 1985), 63.
18. "A 'Seeing' Through Refraction," *Sagetrieb* 10, nos. 1–2 (Spring and Fall 1991), 87.
19. *Poetry* XXXVII, no. 6 (March 1931), 329.
20. *Poetry* XXXVII, no. 6 (March 1931), 333.
21. Simon dissertation, 111–112.
22. U.S. Bureau of Labor Statistics.
23. *New York Times,* early February 1931.
24. In *On Native Grounds,* Alfred Kazin points to the decline of the novel during the 1930s as evidence of this trend.
25. *Made in America,* 144.
26. Holly Stevens, ed., *Letters of Wallace Stevens,* 288.
27. See Williams's editorial comment in the inaugural edition of *Contact* 1, no. 1 (February 1932).
28. Cited in Goldstein, *The American Poet at the Movies,* 136.
29. *American Writers' Congress,* 118.
30. Herman Spector in *Dynamo: A Journal of Revolutionary Poetry,* 1934.
31. Dembo interview, 170.
32. Dembo interview, 174.
33. Stott, 128–134.
34. Letter to the author, 6 July 1996.
35. Cowley, 11.
36. Stott, 105.
37. According to Mary McCarthy; see Stott, 75.
38. Stott, 77.
39. Sweet, *Traces of War,* 86.
40. Stange, *Symbols of Ideal Life,* 66.
41. Barthes, 81.
42. "Documentary Photography," in *Photo Notes* (January 1939), 3.
43. See books such as Alain Jaubert's *Making People Disappear: An Amazing Chronicle of Photographic Deception* (Pergamon-Brassey's International Defense Publishers, 1989) and David King's *The Commissar Vanishes: The Falsification of Photographs and Art in Stalin's Russia* (Metropolitan Books, 1997).

44. The Metropolitan Museum of Art first accepted photographs into its permanent collection during the 1930s.
45. Cited in Trachtenberg, *Reading American Photographs,* 234.
46. *Unclassified,* 7.
47. *Walker Evans at Work,* 70.
48. Other photographers who inspired Evans include Eugene Atget, the German photographer August Sander, as well as Paul Strand and Ralph Steiner in the United States.
49. Cited in Coles, *Doing Documentary Work,* 124.
50. *The Hungry Eye,* 11.
51. *New York Sun,* 8 February 1926.
52. *Grierson on Documentary,* 84.
53. *Photography in the Modern Era,* 16.
54. *Photography in the Modern Era,* 28.
55. *Photography in the Modern Era,* 29.
56. *New York Times,* 18 September 1998.
57. *Reading American Photographs,* 241.
58. *Documenting America,* 46.
59. Cited in Curtis, *Mind's Eye, Mind's Truth,* 10.
60. *Photography in the Modern Era,* 35.
61. *On Photography,* 96.
62. Sharp dissertation, 441.
63. "A Few Dont's," *Poetry I,* no. 6 (March 1913).
64. *Ezra Pound: The Image and the Real,* 22.
65. Schneidau, 33.
66. Gombrich, 8.
67. *Selected Letters of George Oppen,* 146.
68. Quoted in Stange, 116.
69. Gombrich, 9.
70. "Politics and Style in Oppen's *Discrete Series,*" *Ironwood* 26, 66.
71. Sieburth, *Instigations,* 121.
72. Rukeyser, 146.
73. *Photography in the Modern Era,* 26.
74. Cited in Bezner, *Photography and Politics in America,* 1.
75. Davis, in Franklin and Steiner, eds. *Mapping American Culture,* 192.
76. "A Backward Glance O'er Travel'd Roads," Blodgett and Bradley, eds., *Leaves of Grass,* 564.
77. Stott, 120.
78. 1855 Preface, Blodgett and Bradley, eds., *Leaves of Grass,* 709.
79. *Reading American Photographs,* 60.
80. *Reading American Photographs,* 67.
81. *Hound & Horn* VII, no. 1 (Oct/Dec 1933), 39.
82. *Reading American Photographs,* 233.

83. "A New Instrument of Vision," in Kostelanetz, 54.
84. *On Photography*, 27.
85. *Connoisseurs of Chaos*, 48.
86. *On Photography*, 28.
87. 1855 Preface, 713.
88. *Doing Documentary Work*, 250.
89. Zukofsky, in *Prepositions*, 167.
90. Dembo interview, 205.
91. Nelson, 127.
92. Stott, 297.

NOTES TO CHAPTER TWO

1. Quoted in *Charles Reznikoff: Man and Poet*, 64.
2. Burke's introduction, xiii.
3. *Ghostlier Demarcations*, 139.
4. Stott, 78.
5. See "The Case of Confused Identity" in *Does the Camera Ever Lie?* http://memory.loc.gov/ammem/cwphtml/cwpcam/cwcam1.html. Library of Congress, American Memory, http://loc.org (11 May 2005).
6. Stott, 61.
7. "Paper Bound Poets," *The New York Evening Post*, 14 August 1920, cited in *Man and Poet*, 416.
8. *Man and Poet*, 155.
9. "History and Objectification in Charles Reznikoff's Documentary Poems, *Testimony* and *Holocaust*," *Sagetrieb* 1, no. 2 (Fall 1982), 290.
10. Elizabeth McCausland, "Documentary Photography," in *Photo League* (January 1939).
11. Dembo interview, 193.
12. See, for instance, Kathryn Shevelow's "History and Objectification in Charles Reznikoff's Documentary Poems, *Testimony* and *Holocaust*," *Sagetrieb* 1, no. 2 (Fall 1982); Janet Sutherland's essay "Reznikoff and His Sources" from *Man and Poet*; and Michael Davidson's *Ghostlier Demarcations: Modern Poetry and the Material World*.
13. Cited in *Man and Poet*, 420.
14. "Reznikoff's Nearness," *Sulfur* 32 (Spring 1993), 21.
15. *Man and Poet*, 64.
16. See, for example, essays by Charles Bernstein, Linda Simon, L. S. Dembo, and Randolph Chilton in *Charles Reznikoff: Man and Poet*.
17. *Man and Poet*, 130.
18. Kathryn Shevelow, "History and Objectification in Charles Reznikoff's Documentary Poems, *Testimony* and *Holocaust*," in *Sagetrieb* 1, no. 2 (Fall 1982), 292.

19. *Poetry* XXXVII, no. 5 (February 1931), 283.
20. *Poetry* XXXVII, no. 5 (February 1931), 283.
21. "Reznikoff's Nearness," *Sulfur* 32 (Spring 1993), 12.
22. *Shifting Gears*, 211.
23. Cited in Rabinowitz, 96.
24. *Doing Documentary Work*, 236.
25. *Man and Poet*, 131.
26. Milton Hindus, ed., *Selected Letters of Charles Reznikoff 1917–1976*, 101.
27. *Man and Poet*, 276.
28. Cited in *Man and Poet*, 112.
29. William Stott, *Documentary Expression and Thirties America*, 135.
30. See Stott, 134.
31. Paul Strand, whose camera work influenced Evans, was one of Hine's students there.
32. *Reading American Photographs*, 203.
33. Cited in *Man and Poet*, 416.
34. Stott, 30.
35. *Reading American Photographs*, 196.
36. Rabinowitz, 9.
37. *Conviction's Net of Branches*, 69.
38. Sutherland, "Reznikoff and His Sources," 306.
39. Bird, *The Invisible Scar*, 194.
40. *Contact* 1, no. 2 (May 1932), 132.
41. Oppen often misquoted these lines as "*the* girder...among the *rubble*"—see Robert Franciosi's "Reading Reznikoff: Zukofsky, Oppen, and Niedecker" in *The Objectivist Nexus*.
42. *Conviction's Net of Branches*, 60.
43. *Hound & Horn* VII, no. 4 (July-September 1934), 739.

NOTES TO CHAPTER THREE

1. Schimmel, in *George Oppen: Man and Poet*, 294.
2. Interview with L. S. Dembo in *Contemporary Literature* 10 (Spring 1969), 163—referred to hereafter as Dembo interview.
3. *On Native Grounds*, 492.
4. In *George Oppen: Man and Poet*, 300.
5. *New Collected Poems*, 129. Note: Most citations from Oppen's poetry are from this text, hereafter abbreviated as *NCP*, unless otherwise indicated.
6. *The Selected Letters of George Oppen*, 38.
7. *Selected Letters*, 144.
8. Dembo interview, 174.
9. Reed, "A Son Rebels," 8.
10. "The New Poetical Economy" in *Something to Say*, 58.

11. *Selected Letters,* 254.
12. *Selected Letters,* 82.
13. Cited in *Man and Poet,* 464.
14. *Selected Letters,* 90.
15. *Man and Poet,* 93.
16. "The New Conditions of Literary Phenomena," *Broom* 2 (1922), 6.
17. Mumford, 363.
18. Mumford, 350.
19. Eliot Weinberger, "A Little Heap for George Oppen," *Paideuma* 10, no. 9 (1981), 131.
20. "Saccadic movement, the eyes' prime technique for exploring visual space and perceiving shapes and relationships—well-documented since the 1930s. . . ." (see Collins, *The Poetics of the Mind's Eye,* 98).
21. Dembo interview, 201.
22. Cited in *Conviction's Net of Branches,* 3.
23. See, for instance, Tom Sharp's "George Oppen, *Discrete Series,* 1929–1934" in *Man and Poet.*
24. In *NCP,* 360.
25. *Made in America,* 40.
26. Interview with David McAleavey in "Oppen on Oppen," *Sagetrieb* 5, (Spring 1986), 68.
27. *Sulfur* 25 (Fall 1989), 16.
28. Cited in *Man and Poet,* 205.
29. *Selected Letters,* 241.
30. See Tom Sharp in *Man and Poet,* 279, for another opinion.
31. *Selected Letters,* 241.
32. Cited in *Man and Poet,* 279.
33. *Man and Poet,* 279.
34. *Selected Letters,* 156.
35. *Ironwood* 26 (Fall 1985), 14–15.
36. Power, "An Interview with George and Mary Oppen," *Montemora* 4 (1978), 200.
37. Tom Sharp, cited in *Man and Poet,* 288.
38. *Ironwood* 26 (Fall 1985), 16.
39. *Meaning a Life,* 134–135; see also *Selected Letters,* note 404.
40. *Meaning a Life,* 68.
41. *Meaning a Life,* 144.
42. Kenner, "The Poem as Lens," 166.
43. Kenner, 166.
44. Kenner, 167.
45. Kenner, 168.
46. Kenner, 166.
47. Stott, 8.
48. Cited in Stott, 12.

49. Stott, 9.
50. *Conviction's Net of Branches*, 5.
51. Schneidau, *Ezra Pound: The Image and the Real*, 21.
52. *Selected Letters*, 257.
53. Stott, 184.
54. Dembo interview, 168.
55. In DuPlessis, ed., "The Anthropologist of Myself," *Sulfur* 26 (Spring 1990), 149, from Oppen's working papers.
56. *The Dance of the Intellect*, 128.
57. *Selected Letters*, 254.
58. Cited in *Man and Poet*, 257.
59. "Politics and Style in Oppen's *Discrete Series*," *Ironwood* 26 (Fall 1985), 63.
60. *Selected Letters* 122.
61. *Selected Letters*, 122.
62. *Meaning a Life*, 89.
63. *Poetic Closure*, 99.
64. From Oppen's working papers, see *Sulfur* 25 (Fall 1989), 16.
65. *Selected Letters*, 254.
66. Cited in Stott, 76.
67. Cited in Heller, *Conviction's Net of Branches*, 9.

NOTES TO CHAPTER FOUR

1. Schmidt in *WCW, the Arts, and Literary Tradition*, 6.
2. John C. Thirlwall, ed., *The Selected Letters of William Carlos Williams*, 138.
3. *I Wanted to Write a Poem*, 52.
4. H. R. Hays in *Hound & Horn* VII, no. 4 (July-September 1934), 737–738.
5. *Selected Letters*, 102.
6. Cited in Dijkstra, *A Recognizable Image*, 1.
7. Cited in *WCW: The Critical Heritage*, 130.
8. *Opus Posthumous*, 258.
9. *Cubism, Stieglitz, and the Early Poetry of William Carlos Williams*, 165.
10. *William Carlos Williams*, 430.
11. "Program: 'Objectivists' 1931," *Poetry* (February 1931), 268.
12. *Autobiography*, 264–265.
13. *Prepositions*, 149.
14. Ahearn, ed., *Pound/Zukofsky*, 7.
15. *Autobiography*, 391.
16. *Prepositions*, 148.
17. *Selected Essays*, 256.
18. *Shifting Gears*, xiii.
19. Wagner, ed., *Speaking Straight Ahead*, 69.
20. See Doyle in *WCW, the Critical Heritage*, 169.

21. *The Symposium* IV, no. 1 (January 1933), 114.
22. See Stanley Archer essay (1976) cited in *Man and Poet,* 497.
23. *Selected Essays,* 256.
24. *A Homemade World,* 58.
25. *I Wanted to Write a Poem,* 37.
26. Preface to *Collected Poems 1921–1931,* 1.
27. *I Wanted to Write a Poem,* 52.
28. *Selected Essays,* 256.
29. Cited in Coles, *Doing Documentary Work,* 204.
30. *Doing Documentary Work,* 135.
31. *Shifting Gears,* 280.
32. Tichi, 281.
33. Williams received the Dial Award in 1926 for an early version of *Paterson.*
34. *I Wanted to Write a Poem,* 73.
35. "Sermon with a Camera," *New York Times,* 12 October 1938, Williams's review of Evans's book *American Photographs.*
36. Dijkstra, *A Recognizable Image,* 136–137.
37. "Sermon with a Camera."
38. Coles, 131–132.
39. *Cubism, Stieglitz, and the Early Poetry of WCW,* 48.
40. "Photography and the New God," in *Broom* 3 (November 1922), 252–258.
41. Cited in Dijkstra, *Cubism,* 99.
42. *Adventures in the Arts,* 106–107.
43. *Adventures in the Arts,* 108–109.
44. *Adventures in the Arts,* 106.
45. Cited in Dijkstra, *Cubism,* 102.
46. *WCW, the Arts, and Literary Tradition,* 15.
47. *Quality: Its Image in the Arts,* 206.
48. Dijkstra, *A Recognizable Image,* 36.
49. *A Recognizable Image,* 30–31.
50. *WCW & Others,* 116.
51. *Cubism, Stieglitz, and the Early Poetry of William Carlos Williams,* 172.
52. *Cubism,* 190–191.
53. *The Dance of the Intellect,* 120.
54. Bird, *The Invisible Scar,* 154.
55. Pound in the preface to *Discrete Series,* in *George Oppen: New Collected Poems,* 4.
56. Cited in *Charles Reznikoff: Man and Poet,* 31–32.
57. Cited in *Charles Reznikoff: Man and Poet,* 131.
58. Reznikoff, from "Early History of a Writer" in *By the Well of Living & Seeing,* 131.
59. Fiero, 974–975.
60. *I Wanted to Write a Poem,* 72–73.

61. *I Wanted to Write a Poem,* 72.
62. Bram Dijkstra, Marjorie Perloff, Andrew Clearfield, Henry Sayre, and George Layng are a few of those who have written about the influence of Cubism on Williams's writing.
63. *Ghostlier Demarcations,* 139.
64. *A Recognizable Image,* 18.
65. *Imaginations,* 88.
66. *Imaginations,* 89.
67. Blodgett and Bradley, eds., *Leaves of Grass,* 717.
68. *Imaginations,* 89.
69. Zukofsky, *Prepositions,* 194.
70. "Sermon with a Camera," *New York Times,* 12 October 1938.

Bibliography

BOOKS

Aaron, Daniel. *Writers on the Left: Episodes in American Literary Communism.* New York: Harcourt, Brace & World, 1961.

Adorno, Theodor W. *Notes to Literature,* vol. 1. New York: Columbia University Press, 1991.

Agee, James and Walker Evans. *Let Us Now Praise Famous Men.* Boston: Houghton Mifflin, 1941.

Ahearn, Barry, ed. *The Correspondence of William Carlos Williams and Louis Zukofsky.* Middletown, CT: Wesleyan University Press, 2003.

——. *Pound/Zukofsky: Selected Letters of Ezra Pound and Louis Zukofsky.* New York: New Directions, 1987.

Allerte, Beate, ed. *Languages of Visuality: Crossings between Science, Art, Politics and Literature.* Detroit: Wayne State University Press, 1996.

Ardizzone, Maria Luisa, ed. *Machine Art and Other Writings: The Lost Thought of the Italian Years—Ezra Pound.* Durham and London: Duke University Press, 1996.

Barrett, Terry. *Criticizing Photographs.* Mountain View, CA: Mayfield Publishing Company, 1996.

Barthes, Roland. *Camera Lucida.* New York: Hill and Wang, 1981.

Bezner, Lili Corbus. *Photography and Politics in America: from the New Deal into the Cold War.* Baltimore: Johns Hopkins University Press, 1999.

Blodgett, Harold W. and Sculley Bradley, eds. *Walt Whitman: Leaves of Grass.* New York: W.W. Norton and Company, 1965.

Bogardus, Ralph F. and Fred Hobson, eds. *Literature at the Barricades: The American Writer in the 1930s.* University, AL: University of Alabama Press, 1982.

Bové, Paul A. *Destructive Poetics: Heidegger and Modern American Poetry.* New York: Columbia University Press, 1980.

Breslin, James E. B., ed. *Something to Say: William Carlos Williams on Younger Poets.* New York: New Directions, 1985.

Bryant, Marsha. *Auden and Documentary in the 1930s.* Charlottesville: University Press of Virginia, 1997.

Childs, John Steven. *Modernist Form: Pound's Style in the Early Cantos.* Selinsgrove, PA: Susquehanna University Press, 1986.

Cirasa, Robert J. *The Lost Works of William Carlos Williams: The Volumes of Collected Poetry as Lyrical Sequences.* London: Associated University Presses, 1995.

Clearfield, Andrew M. *These Fragments I Have Shored: Collage and Montage in Early Modernist Poetry.* Ann Arbor: UMI Research Press, 1984.

Coben, Stanley and Lorman Ratner, eds. *The Development of an American Culture.* Englewood Cliffs, NJ: Prentice Hall, 1970.

Coffman, Jr., Stanley K. *Imagism: A Chapter for the History of Modern Poetry.* Norman, OK: University of Oklahoma Press, 1951.

Coles, Robert. *Doing Documentary Work.* New York, Oxford: Oxford University Press, 1997.

Collins, Christopher. *The Poetics of the Mind's Eye.* Philadelphia: University of Pennsylvania Press, 1991.

Cowley, Malcolm. *Exile's Return: A Literary Odyssey of the 1920s.* New York: Viking Penguin, 1951.

Cummings, Paul. *Artists in Their Own Words.* New York: St. Martin's Press, 1979.

Curtis, James. *Mind's Eye, Mind's Truth: FSA Photography Reconsidered.* Philadelphia: Temple University Press, 1989.

Davidson, Michael. *Ghostlier Demarcations: Modern Poetry and the Material World.* Berkeley, Los Angeles, London: University of California Press, 1997.

Davie, Donald. *Articulate Energy.* London: Routledge & Kegan Paul, 1955.

Dembo, L. S. *Conceptions of Reality in Modern American Poetry.* Berkeley and Los Angeles: University of California Press, 1966.

DeNoon, Christopher. *Posters of the WPA.* Los Angeles: The Wheatley Press, 1987.

Dijkstra, Bram. *Cubism, Stieglitz, and the Early Poetry of William Carlos Williams.* Princeton: Princeton University Press, 1969.

Dijkstra, Bram, ed. *A Recognizable Image: William Carlos Williams on Art and Artists.* New York: New Directions, 1978.

Donoghue, Denis. *Connoisseurs of Chaos: Ideas of Order in Modern American Poetry.* New York: Columbia University Press, 1984.

Doyle, Charles, ed. *William Carlos Williams: The Critical Heritage.* London, Boston, and Henley: Routledge & Kegan Paul, 1980.

DuPlessis, Rachel Blau. *The Selected Letters of George Oppen.* Durham and London: Duke University Press, 1990.

DuPlessis, Rachel Blau and Peter Quartermain, eds. *The Objectivist Nexus: Essays in Cultural Poetics.* Tuscaloosa and London: University of Alabama Press, 1999.

Eagleton, Terry. *Literary Theory: An Introduction.* Minneapolis: University of Minnesota Press, 1983.

Eisinger, Joel. *Trace and Transformation.* Albuquerque: University of New Mexico Press, 1995.

Eliot, T. S. *Literary Essays of Ezra Pound.* New York: New Directions, 1954.

Ellis, Jack C. *The Documentary Idea: A Critical History of English-language Documentary Film and Video.* Englewood Cliffs, NJ: Prentice Hall, 1989.

Evans, Walker. *The Hungry Eye.* New York: Harry N. Abrams, 1993.

——. *Walker Evans at Work.* New York: Harper and Row, 1982.

Featherstone, David, ed. *Observations.* Carmel, CA: Friends of Photography, 1984.

Felman, Shoshana and Dori Laub, MD. *Testimony: Crises of Witnessing in Literature, Psychoanalysis, and History.* New York and London: Routledge, 1992.

Filreis, Alan. *Modernism from Right to Left: Wallace Stevens, the Thirties, and Literary Radicalism.* Cambridge: Cambridge University Press, 1994.

——. *Wallace Stevens and the Actual World.* Princeton: Princeton University Press, 1991.

Finnegan, Cara A. *Picturing Poverty: Print Culture and FSA Photographs.* Washington, D.C.: Smithsonian Institution Press, 2003.

Fleischhauer, Carl and Beverly W. Brannan, eds. *Documenting America, 1935–1943.* Berkeley: University of California, 1988.

Franklin, Wayne and Michael Steiner, eds. *Mapping American Culture.* Iowa City: University of Iowa Press, 1992.

Galassi, Peter. *Walker Evans & Company.* New York: The Museum of Modern Art, 2000.

Goldstein, Laurence. *The American Poet at the Movies.* Ann Arbor: University of Michigan Press, 1994.

Gombrich, E. H. *Meditations on a Hobby horse, and Other Essays on the Theory of Art.* London: Phaidon, 1963.

Gray, Richard. *American Poetry of the Twentieth Century.* London and New York, 1990.

Gregory, Elizabeth. *Quotation and Modern American Poetry.* Houston: Rice University Press, 1996.

Greif, Martin. *Depression Modern: The Thirties Style in America.* New York: Universe Books, 1975.

Grundberg, Andy. *Crisis of the Real.* New York: Aperture Foundation, 1990.

Hardy, Forsyth, ed. *Grierson on Documentary.* London and Boston: Faber and Faber, 1979.

Hart, Henry. *American Writers' Congress.* New York: International Publishers, 1935.

Hartley, Marsden. *Adventures in the Arts.* New York: Hacker Art Books, 1972 (first published 1921).

Hartman, Geoffrey H. *The Unmediated Vision: An Interpretation of Wordsworth, Hopkins, Rilke, and Valéry.* New Haven: Yale University Press, 1954.

Hatlen, Burton, ed. *George Oppen: Man and Poet.* Orono, ME: National Poetry Foundation, 1981.

Hatlen, Burton and Demetros Tryphonopoulos, eds. *William Carlos Williams and the Language of Poetry.* Orono, ME: National Poetry Foundation, 2002.

Heidegger, Martin. *Poetry Language Thought* (trans. and intro. by Albert Hofstadter). New York: Harper and Row, 1971.

Heller, Michael, ed. *Carl Rakosi: Man and Poet.* Orono, ME: National Poetry Foundation, 1993.

Heller, Michael. *Conviction's Net of Branches.* Carbondale and Edwardsville: Southern Illinois University Press, 1985.

Hicks, Granville, Joseph North, Michael Gold, Paul Peters, Isidor Schneider, and Alan Calmer, eds. *Proletarian Literature in the United States.* New York: International Publishers, 1935.

Hindus, Milton, ed. *Charles Reznikoff: Man and Poet.* Orono, ME: National Poetry Foundation, 1984.

——. *Selected Letters of Charles Reznikoff 1917–1976.* Santa Rosa: Black Sparrow Press, 1997.

Homberger, Eric. *American Writers and Radical Politics 1900–39 Equivocal Commitments.* Hampshire and London: Macmillan Press, 1986.

——. *The Art of the Real: Poetry in England and America Since 1939.* Dent, London, and Toronto: Rowman and Littlefield, Totowa, NJ, 1977.

Hurley, F. Jack. *Portrait of a Decade: Roy Stryker and the Development of Documentary Photography in the Thirties.* Baton Rouge: Louisiana State University, 1972.

Jacobs, Karen. *The Eye's Mind: Literary Modernism and Visual Culture.* Ithaca, NY: Cornell University Press, 2001.

Jones, Manina. *That Art of Difference: "Documentary-Collage" and English Canadian Writing.* Toronto: University of Toronto Press, 1993.

Kazin, Alfred. *On Native Grounds, an Interpretation of Modern American Prose Literature.* San Diego: Harcourt Brace Jovanovich, 1982.

Kemp, John R., ed. *Lewis Hine: Photographs of Child Labor in the New South.* Jackson, MS: University Press of Mississippi, 1986.

Kenner, Hugh. *A Homemade World: the American Modernist Writers.* Baltimore: Johns Hopkins University Press, 1989.

——. *The Pound Era.* Berkeley: University of California Press, 1973.

Kertesz, Louise. *The Poetic Vision of Muriel Rukeyser.* Baton Rouge and London: Louisiana State University Press, 1980.

Kostelanetz, Richard. *Moholy-Nagy.* New York, Washington: Praeger Publishers, 1970.

Kronenberger, Louis, ed. *Quality: Its Image in the Arts.* New York: Atheneum, 1969.

Larrissey, Edward. *Reading Twentieth-Century Poetry: The Language of Gender and Objects.* Oxford and Cambridge, MA: Basil Blackwell, 1990.

Levitt, Helen. *A Way of Seeing.* Durham and London: Duke University Press, 1989.

MacGowan, Christopher. *William Carlos Williams's Early Poetry: The Visual Arts Background.* Ann Arbor: UMI Research Press, 1984.

Mao, Douglas. *Solid Objects: Modernism and the Test of Production.* Princeton: Princeton University Press, 1998.

Mariani, Paul. *William Carlos Williams: A New World Naked.* New York: McGraw-Hill, 1981.

——. *William Carlos Williams: The Poet and His Critics.* Chicago: New American Library Association, 1975.

McAleavey, David. "If to Know Is Noble: The Poetry of George Oppen." Diss. Cornell, 1975.

McEven, Melissa A. *Seeing America: Women Photographers Between the Wars.* Lexington: University Press of Kentucky, 2000.

McGann, Jerome. *Black Riders: The Visible Language of Modernism.* Princeton: Princeton University Press, 1993.

Miller, Hillis J. *Poets of Reality.* Cambridge, MA: Belknap Press, 1965.

Mumford, Lewis. *Technics and Civilization.* New York: Harcourt, Brace & Co., 1934.

Nelson, Cary. *Repression and Recovery: Modern American Poetry and the Politics of Cultural Memory 1910–1945.* Madison, WA: University of Wisconsin Press, 1989.

Newhall, Beaumont, ed. *Photography: Essays and Images—Illustrated Readings in the History of Photography.* New York: Museum of Modern Art, 1980.

North, Michael. *Camera Works: Photography and the Twentieth-Century Word.* New York: Oxford University Press, 2004.

Oliphant, Dave and Thomas Zigel. *WCW & Others.* The University of Texas at Austin: Harry Ranson Humanities Research Center, 1985.

Oppen, George. *Collected Poems.* New York: New Directions Books, 1975.

——. *New Collected Poems.* New York, New Directions Books, 2002.

Oppen, Mary. *Meaning a Life.* Santa Barbara: Black Sparrow Press, 1978.

Pells, Richard H. *Radical Visions and American Dreams: Culture and Social Thought in the Depression Years.* Middletown, CT: Wesleyan University Press, 1973.

Perloff, Marjorie. *The Dance of the Intellect: Studies in the Poetry of the Pound Tradition.* Cambridge, London, New York, New Rochelle, Melbourne, Sydney: Cambridge University Press, 1985.

——. *Radical Artifice.* Chicago and London: University of Chicago Press, 1991.

Phillips, Christopher, ed. *Photography in the Modern Era: European Documents and Critical Writings, 1913–1940.* New York: Aperture, 1989.

Pound, Ezra. *ABC of Reading.* London: G. Routledge & Sons, 1934.

——. *Make It New* (essays). New Haven: Yale University Press, 1935.

——. *Polite Essays.* Norwalk, CT: New Directions, n.d.

Puckett, John Rogers. *Five Photo-Textual Documentaries from the Great Depression.* Ann Arbor, Michigan: UMI Research Press, 1984.

Rabate, Jean-Michel, ed. *Writing the Image After Roland Barthes.* Philadelphia: University of Pennsylvania Press, 1997.

Rabinowitz, Paula. *They Must Be Represented: The Politics of Documentary.* London, New York: Verso, 1994.

Rahv, Philip. *Image and Idea.* Norwalk, CT: New Directions, 1949.

Rainey, Lawrence S. *Ezra Pound and the Monument of Culture.* Chicago: University of Chicago Press, 1991.

Rakosi, Carl. *Poems 1923–1941.* Los Angeles: Sun and Moon Press, 1995.

Renov, Michael, ed. *Theorizing Documentary.* Routledge: New York and London, 1993.

Reznikoff, Charles. *By the Waters of Manhattan.* New York: New Directions, 1962.

——. *By the Well of Living and Seeing, New and Selected Poems 1918–1973.* Los Angeles: Black Sparrow Press, 1974.

——. *The Complete Poem of Charles Reznikoff,* vol. 1 (Poems 1918–1936), Seamus Cooney, ed. Santa Barbara: Black Sparrow Press, 1976.

——. *Holocaust.* Los Angeles: Black Sparrow Press, 1975.

——. *Testimony.* New York: The Objectivist Press, 1934.

——. *Testimony, Vol. I The United States (1885–1915) Recitative.* Santa Barbara: Black Sparrow Press, 1978.

——. *Testimony, Vol. II The United States (1885–1915) Recitative.* Santa Barbara: Black Sparrow Press, 1979.

Rosenblatt, Louise M. *The Reader the Text the Poem: the Transactional Theory of the Literary Work.* Carbondale and Edwardsville: Southern Illinois University Press, 1978.

Rosenheim, Jeff L. and Douglas Eklund. *Unclassified: A Walker Evans Anthology.* Zurich: Scalo-Zurich—Berlin—New York, 2000.

Roskill, Mark and David Carrier. *Truth and Falsehood in Visual Images.* Amherst: The University of Massachusetts Press, 1983.

Rukeyser, Muriel. *U.S. 1.* New York: Covici Friede, 1938.

Sandburg, Carl. *The People, Yes.* New York: Harcourt Brace, 1936.

Sayre, Henry M. *The Visual Text of William Carlos Williams.* Urbana and Chicago: University of Illinois Press, 1983.

Schmidt, Peter. *William Carlos Williams, the Arts, and Literary Tradition.* Baton Rouge and London: Louisiana State University Press, 1988.

Schneidau, Herbert N. *Ezra Pound: The Image and the Real.* Baton Rouge: Louisiana State University Press, 1969.

Schott, Webster, ed. *William Carlos Williams: Imaginations.* New York: New Directions, 1970.

Scroggins, Mark. *Louis Zukofsky and the Poetry of Knowledge.* Tuscaloosa: University of Alabama Press, 1998.

Sharp, Fred Thomas. "'Objectivists' 1927–1934." Diss. Stanford, 1982.

Simon, Linda. "The Making of Objectivists." Diss. Brandeis, 1983.

Smith, Barbara Herrnstein. *Poetic Closure: A Study of How Poems End.* Chicago: University of Chicago Press, 1968.

Sontag, Susan. *On Photography.* New York: Farrar, Straus, and Giroux, 1973.

Stange, Maren. *Symbols of Ideal Life: Social Documentary Photography in America 1890–1950.* Cambridge: Cambridge University Press, 1989.

Stanley, Sandra Kumamoto. *Louis Zukofsky and the Transformation of Modern American Poetics.* Berkeley: University of California Press, 1994.

Steinman, Lisa M. *Made in America: Science, Technology, and American Modernist Poets.* New Haven and London: Yale University Press, 1987.

Steinorth, Karl, ed. *Lewis Hine: Passionate Journey, Photographs 1905–1937.* Zurich: Edition Stemmle, 1996.

Stevens, Wallace. *Opus Posthumous.* New York: Alfred A. Knopf, 1957.

Stott, William. *Documentary Expression and Thirties America.* Chicago and London: University of Chicago Press, 1986.

Sweet, Timothy. *Traces of War: Poetry, Photography, and the Crisis of the Union.* Baltimore and London: Johns Hopkins University Press, 1990.

Szarkowski, John. *The Photographer's Eye.* New York: Doubleday, 1966.

Tashjian, Dickran. *Skyscraper Primitives: Dada and the American Avant-garde 1910–1925.* Middletown, CT: Wesleyan University Press 1975.

Teitelbaum, Matthew, ed. *Montage and Modern Life 1919–1942.* Cambridge, MA, and London: The MIT Press, 1992.

Terrell, Carroll F., ed. *Louis Zukofsky: Man and Poet.* Orono, ME: National Poetry Foundation, 1978.

——. *William Carlos Williams: Man and Poet.* Orono, ME: National Poetry Foundation, 1983.

Thirlwall, John C., ed. *The Selected Letters of William Carlos Williams.* New York: McDowell, Obolensky, 1957.

Tichi, Cecelia. *Shifting Gears: Technology, Literature, Culture in Modernist America.* Chapel Hill and London: University of North Carolina Press, 1987.

Tomlinson, Charles, ed. *William Carlos Williams: Selected Poems.* New York: New Directions, 1985.

Trachtenberg, Alan. *Reading American Photographs.* Hill and Wang, 1989.

von Hallberg, Robert. *Charles Olson: The Scholar's Art.* Cambridge, MA; London: Harvard University Press, 1978.

Wagner, Linda Welshimer, ed. *"Speaking Straight Ahead": Interviews with Williams Carlos Williams.* New York: New Directions, 1976.

Williams, Keith and Steven Matthews, eds. *Rewriting the Thirties: Modernism and After.* London and New York: Longman, 1997.

Williams, William Carlos. *The Autobiography of William Carlos Williams.* New York: New Directions, 1948.

——. *The Collected Earlier Poems of William Carlos Williams.* New York: New Directions, 1951.

——. *Collected Poems 1921–1931.* New York: The Objectivist Press, 1934.

——. *The Embodiment of Knowledge.* New York, New Directions, 1974.

——. *I Wanted to Write a Poem.* Boston: Beacon Press, 1958.

——. *In the American Grain.* With an introduction by Horace Gregory. Norwalk, CT: New Directions, 1925.

——. *Paterson.* New York: New Directions, 1946.

——. *Selected Essays of William Carlos Williams.* New York: Random House, 1954.

Wilson, Edmund. *Axel's Castle.* New York, London: C. Scribner's Sons, 1931.

Wilson, Richard Guy, Dianne H. Pilgrim, amd Dickran Tashjian. *The Machine Age in America 1918–1941.* New York: Harry N. Abrams, 1986.

Zinnes, Harriet, ed. *Ezra Pound and the Visual Arts.* New York: New Directions, 1980.

Zukofsky, Louis. *ALL the collected short poems 1923–1958*. London: Jonathan Cape, 1965.

——. *Complete Short Poetry*. Baltimore and London: Johns Hopkins University Press, 1991.

——. *Prepositions: The Collected Critical Essays of Louis Zukofsky*. Berkeley: University of California, 1981.

JOURNAL ARTICLES AND PERIODICALS

Altieri, Charles. "The Objectivist Tradition." *Chicago Review* 30, no. 3 (Winter 1979): 5–22.

Bazin, André. "The Ontology of the Photographic Image." In Peninah R. Petruck, ed., *The Camera Viewed: Writings on Twentieth-Century Photography*, vol. 2 (New York: E. P. Dutton, 1979): 140–146.

Beebe, Maurice. "What Modernism Was." *Journal of Modern Literature* 3, no. 5 (July 1974): 1065–1084.

Bergan, Brooke. "A Wedge in Time: the Poetics of Photography." *Antioch Review* 48, no. 4 (Fall 1990): 509–524.

Bernstein, Charles. "Reznikoff's Nearness." *Sulfur* 32 (Spring 1993): 6–40.

Cole, Peter. "The Object and Its Edge: Rothko, Oppen, Zukofsky, and Newman." *Sagetrieb* 5, no. 3 (1986): 127–145.

Contact 1, nos. 1 (February 1932) and 2 (May 1932).

Davidson, Michael. "Forms of Refusal: George Oppen's 'Distant Life.'" *Sulfur* 26 (Spring 1990): 127–133.

Dembo, L. S. "The Existential World of George Oppen." *Iowa Review* 3 (1972): 64–91.

——. "The 'Objectivist' Poet: Four Interviews." *Contemporary Literature* 10, no. 2 (Spring 1969): 155–219.

Does the Camera Ever Lie? http://memory.loc.gov/ammem/cwphtml /cwpcam/ cwcam1.html. Library of Congress, American Memory, http://loc.org (11 May 2005).

DuPlessis, Rachel Blau, ed. "The Anthropologist of Myself: A Selection From Working Papers." *Sulfur* 26 (Spring 1990): 135–164.

——. "The Circumstances: A Selection from George Oppen's Uncollected Writing." *Sulfur* 25 (Fall 1989): 10–43.

——. "The Philosophy of the Astonished (Selections from the Working Papers of George Oppen)." *Sulfur* 27 (Fall 1990): 202–220.

Dynamo: A Journal of Revolutionary Poetry (1934).

Epstein, Jean. "The New Conditions of Literary Phenomena." *Broom* 2, no. 1 (April 1922): 3–10.

Feld, Ross. "Some Thought About Objectivism." *Sagetrieb* 12, no. 3 (Winter 1993): 65–77.

Fiero, F. Douglass. "Williams Creates the First Book of *Paterson.*" *Journal of Modern Literature* 3, no. 4 (April 1974): 965–984.

Flint, F. S. "Imagisme." *Poetry* I, no. 6 (March 1913): 198–200.

Golding, Alan. "Politics and Style in George Oppen's *Discrete Series.*" *Ironwood* 26 (Fall 1985): 62–68.

Holsapple, Bruce. "Poetic Design in Reznikoff's *Testimony.*" *Sagetrieb 13,* no. 1 (Spring 1994): 123–145.

Hound & Horn VII, nos. 1 (October/December 1933) and 4 (July 1934—final issue).

Ironwood 26: George Oppen, A Special Issue. Vol. 13, no. 2 (Fall 1985).

Kaufman, Shirley. "Charles Reznikoff, 1894–1976: An Appreciation." *Midstream* (August/September 1976): 51–56.

Kronick, Joseph G. "George Oppen's Life and Career." *American National Biography* (New York: Oxford University Press, 1999).

Lavery, David. "Poetry as Time-Lapse Photography." *Essays in Arts and Sciences* 17 (May 1988): 1–27.

Levine, Lawrence W. "American Culture and the Great Depression." *Yale Review* 74 (Winter 1985): 196–223.

Lunberry, Clark. "So Much Depends: Printed Matter, Dying Words, and the Entropic Poem." *Critical Inquiry* 30, no. 3 (Spring 2004): 627–653.

McAleavey, David. "A Bibliography of the Works of George Oppen." *Paideuma* 10, no. 9 (1981): 155–169.

——. "Oppen on Oppen: Extracts from Interviews." *Sagetrieb* 5, no. 1 (Spring 1986): 59–93.

McCausland, Elizabeth. "Documentary Photography." *Photo Notes* (January 1939), http://newdeal.feri.org/pn/pn139.htm, *New Deal Network,* http://newdeal.feri.org (8 May 2005).

——. "Hine's Photo Documents." *Photo Notes* (September 1940), http://newdeal.feri.org/pn/pn940.htm, *New Deal Network,* http://newdeal. feri.org (5 June 2005).

Ming-Qian Ma. "A 'Seeing' Through Refraction: The Rearview Mirror Image in George Oppen's *Collected Poems.*" *Sagetrieb* 10, nos. 1–2 (Spring and Fall 1991): 83–97.

Oppen, George. "Statement on Poetics." *Sagetrieb* 3, no. 3 (Winter 1984): 25–27.

Oppen, George and Mary (interviewed by Charles Amirkhanian). Memorial Broadcast for Charles Reznikoff, KPFA, Berkeley, California. *Sagetrieb* 3, no. 3 (Winter 1984): 29–35.

Paideuma 10, no. 1 (Spring 1981). Special Issue: George Oppen.

Palmer, Michael. "On Objectivism." *Sulfur* 26 (Spring 1990): 117–125.

Parlej, Piotr. "Testing the Image: The Double Interrogative in the Poetry of George Oppen." *Sagetrieb* 10, nos. 1–2 (Spring and Fall 1991): 67–81.

Pevear, Richard. "Poetry and Worldlessness." *Hudson Review* 29 (Summer 1976): 305–320.

Poetry I, no. 6 (March 1913).

Poetry XXXVII, no. 5 (February 1931).

Poetry XXXVII, no. 6 (March 1931).

Poetry XXXIX, no. 4 (January 1932).

Power, Kevin. "An Interview with George and Mary Oppen." *Montemora* 4 (1978): 197–203.

Rakosi, Carl. Letter to the author, 5 July 1996.

Reed, Brian. "A Son Rebels: George Oppen's *Discrete Series* as a Response to Pound and Williams." Paper given at session 146, MLA Convention, San Francisco. 27 December 1998.

Rodman, Selden. "The Poetry of Poverty." *Saturday Review of Literature* 24, no. 34 (23 August 1941).

Schaum, Melita. "The Grammar of the Visual: Alvin Langdon Coburn, Ezra Pound, and the Eastern Aesthetic in Early Modernist Photography and Poetry." *Paideuma* 24, nos. 2–3 (Fall-Winter 1995): 79–106.

Schiffer, Reinhold. "Interview with George Oppen." *Sagetrieb* 3, no. 3 (Winter 1984): 9–23.

Sharp, Tom. "The 'Objectivists' Publications." *Sagetrieb* 3, no. 3 (Winter 1984): 41–47.

Shevelow, Kathryn. "History and Objectification in Charles Reznikoff's Documentary Poems, *Testimony* and *Holocaust.*" *Sagetrieb* 1, no. 2 (Fall 1982): 290–306.

Silliman, Ron. "Third-Phase Objectivism." *Paideuma* 10, no. 1 (Spring 1981): 85–89.

Strand, Paul. "Photography and the New God." *Broom* 3 (November 1922): 252–258.

Sweney, Matthew. "Deposition: The First *Testimony* (1934)." *Sagetrieb* 13, nos. 1–2 (Spring and Fall 1994): 217–224.

Wah, Fred. "Is a Door a Word?" *Mosaic* 37, no. 4 (December 2004): 39–70.

Weinfield, Henry. "'A Thousand Threads' and 'The One Thing': Oppen's Vision (A Reply to Ross Feld)." *Sagetrieb* 12, no. 3 (Winter 1993): 79–87.

Williams, William Carlos. "Sermon with a Camera." Review of Walker Evans's show American Photographs at the Museum of Modern Art. *New York Times,* 12 October 1938.

Winters, Yvor. Review of *An "Objectivists" Anthology. Hound & Horn* VI, no. 1 (October-December 1932): 158–160.

Yoon, Hyonyung. "Optics in Walt Whitman's Poetry: The Principles of Poetic Realism." *Nineteenth Century Literature in English* 8, no. 1 (2004): 33–53.

Index

Y

Z

For Product Safety Concerns and Information please contact our EU representative GPSR@taylorandfrancis.com
Taylor & Francis Verlag GmbH, Kaufingerstraße 24, 80331 München, Germany

www.ingramcontent.com/pod-product-compliance
Lightning Source LLC
LaVergne TN
LVHW010915110826
845149LV00013B/2365

* 9 7 8 1 1 3 8 8 1 2 5 3 6 *